EVALUATING ONLINE RESOURCES
WITH
RESEARCH NAVIGATOR

POLITICAL SCIENCE 2004

Melissa Payton
with contributions by William E. Kelly, Ph.D.

PEARSON

Prentice
Hall

UPPER SADDLE RIVER, NJ 07458

Note: Research Navigator™ is continually expanded and updated. The screen shots included in this documentation may not reflect the latest updates. Refer to <http://www.researchnavigator.com/phguide/ to download the most recent documentation in either Microsoft® Word format or Adobe Acrobat® format.

Contents

Chapter 1

An Overview
of Sources

What Are Sources?

When instructors speak of sources, they're usually referring to "outside" sources--materials outside your own knowledge or thinking that contain someone else's ideas. Sources provide information; they let you learn something you did not know before. Examples of legitimate sources include credible information from the Internet, library collections, and the spoken words of experts. They can be in the form of books, newspaper articles, interviews, television and radio programs, websites, maps, online databases, magazines, computer and video images, audiotapes, and academic journals. Sources add authority to what you write and nearly all college research assignments require their use.

Using sources well is the hallmark of sound nonfiction writing. Most research writing involves a combination of print and online sources. Although this guide will focus on online resources, the advice on evaluating sources--determining whether a website offers credible information that meets the standards of academic research--almost always applies to other sources as well.

Later chapters will help you use sources effectively in your writing. Chapter 2 will help you find online sources, use databases and search engines, and evaluate such sources for credibility. While the Internet is a nearly bottomless well of useful and enlightening information, it is also host to websites created by bigots, conspiracy theorists, and extremists--not to mention those who are well-intentioned but misinformed. Chapter 2 will help you sort the academically nutritious wheat from the Internet junk-food chaff.

Chapter 3 will help you avoid plagiarism, a cardinal sin. It will also acquaint you with paraphrasing and summarizing, and how to cite and document sources. Chapter 4 will introduce you to Research Navigator, a new online academic research service, and Chapters 5, 6, and 7 will show you how to use the service's three major databases. Chapter 8 will help you to use Research Navigator in a specific academic discipline.

Primary and Secondary Sources

Primary sources are firsthand evidence, based on your own or someone else's original work or direct observation. They can be documents, records, letters, diaries, novels, poems, short stories, autobiographies, interviews, and journals. This original quality adds to a source's reliability and impact on the reader.

Here is playwright Endesha Ida Mae Holland in her memoir, "From the Mississippi Delta" (1997):

> I was born into the double shotgun house at 114 East Gibb Street. Mama rented both sides of the clapboard house, which stood on raised posts. A confused patch of petunias hugged the ground at the end of the front porch. Inside, the crudely painted walls were peeling and patched with newspaper. The ceiling was so low that I could read "Little Lulu" on the funny pages pasted there. (pp. 19-20)

Holland goes on to describe the cracks in the linoleum floor that offered a view of the earth under the house and the patched roof that let in daylight and rain. Her brief account does more than describe a house: it tells us, indirectly but powerfully, about the poverty she was born into.

Secondary sources report, describe, comment on, or analyze the experiences or work of others. In college, most textbooks are secondary sources. As a piece of evidence, a secondary source is at least once removed from the primary source. It reports on the original work, the direct observation, or the firsthand experience. But it can have great value and impact as a source if the reporter or writer is reliable, either as a result of special experience (a journalist who spent years observing and reporting on the civil rights movement) or special training (a tooth-decay expert with a dental degree).

Newspapers are typical secondary sources. In a three-part series the *New York Times* published in January, 2003, reporters who examined the safety record of an Alabama-based pipe-making company concluded that it was "one of the most dangerous businesses in America." They based their conclusion on primary sources: company and government records and interviews with current and former employees, including plant managers, safety directors, and environmental engineers.

Here is a quote from the story:

> "The people, they're nothing," said Robert S. Rester, a former McWane plant manager who spoke at length about his 24 years with the company. "They're just numbers. You move them in and out. I mean, if they don't do the job, you fire them. If they get hurt, complain about safety, you put a bull's-eye on them." (Barstow & Bergman, Jan. 9, 2003, p. A1)

The *Times*, and most newspapers and magazines, are generally reliable secondary sources--although even highly-regarded publications make errors under the pressure of deadlines or competition. That's why sound research requires more than one source to back up a disputable claim.

Types of Sources

Print Sources

Newspapers, magazines, academic journals, documents, reference works, and personal papers are all print sources, although more and more of them exist in an online form as well.

For college research, the main tool for locating print sources that are not online is still the library. Many times you'll need to use electronic resources, especially the library catalog, to locate the print materials that you need to pull from the library's shelves. One major advantage of libraries: they come equipped with librarians. Reference-desk staffers can help you home in on the topic you need to research, come up with a research strategy, and determine the best tools to use in your research. The "Using Your Library" section of Research Navigator can also help you use a library's vast resources more efficiently.

Online and Database Sources

The Internet offers unlimited opportunities for research. Many print sources-- newspapers, magazines, reference works, academic journals--are available online as well. One advantage of accessing print sources online, of course, is that you have millions of pages originating from across the globe at your fingertips. Another is that you can download and print a copy of an article for your files. Finally, many online-print sources are *searchable*: you can type a keyword into an archive or database to pull up the page you need. (Databases collect and organize content online so that users can find particular information. When did the "The Wizard of Oz" debut, and how many Oscars did it win? The Internet Movie Database, www.imdb.com, will tell you. Searching online databases is a skill of its own that will be covered in the next chapter.)

Online content that is *not* print-based is even more varied. The most useful sites for research usually are informational and have URL addresses that end in **.edu** or **.gov**. "Edu" websites are sponsored by educational institutions, and they may include research results, reference works, subject indexes, and databases useful in many disciplines. "Gov" sites, sponsored by government agencies, offer a trove of primary sources: census information, federal codes and regulations, licensing records, property data, and health statistics. Sites that end in **.org** are sponsored by a nonprofit organization, such as Planned Parenthood, the National Rifle Association, or Mothers Against Drunk Driving. Some "org" sites offer reliable, usable information--but remember that they are usually sponsored by a group or individual that seeks to influence public opinion.

Although most commercial sites (those with **.com** URLs) exist to sell merchandise, some do offer information useful to students and researchers at low or no cost. News sites are an example (www.nytimes.com, www.newsweek.com, www.washingtonpost.com). Most offer free access to at least the previous week's content. Unfortunately, more and more publications are charging for access to their archives--which contain the information most useful for research. Many college departments, however, buy a subscription to fee-charging online publications like the *Wall Street Journal* or news databases like LexisNexus. You will need to get a sign-on and password from your instructor or department office. (The online Research Navigator, www.researchnavigator.com, free with the purchase of any Prentice Hall college textbook, allows one-year access to the *New York Times*, along with searchable databases of academic and general interest publications and World Wide Web sites.)

Chapter 2

How to Find and Evaluate Online Sources

Finding Online Sources

Yes, there is a wealth of information on the Internet. In fact no one knows how many World Wide Web pages exist, because new ones are being created constantly--they number in the millions, certainly, and some say billions. But how do you find the information you need? And how do you make sure it is credible? Anyone with a few technical skills and access to a computer can publish on the Internet. Some sites offer information from experts; many sites are run by amateurs. Some sites are updated frequently; others, not at all.

To search the Web efficiently, it helps to be familiar with several different strategies and use the one that works best for your research topic. The two main vehicles for accessing information through the Internet are **subject directories** and **search engines**, which will be discussed in more detail in this chapter. If you try out several examples of both types, you will quickly find the search method you favor. Also, search engines and subject directories are not uniform in the techniques users must employ to narrow or broaden a search. So if you are comfortable with several methods of searching--using Boolean operators, truncation (or wild cards), and implied operators, also explained in this chapter-- you will be able to switch more easily from one search engine or subject directory to another.

Strategies for Searching the Web

Tailor your search to the scope of the information you are seeking. To do this, you will need to understand **search engines**, **subject directories**, and **specialized databases**. A subject directory will take you through a sequence of Internet subjects. You might start with "history," move to "military history," then to "Civil War history," "Civil War battles," and arrive finally at the Battle of Gettysburg, your goal. Internet search engines locate specific Internet sites devoted to your topic (such as Military History Online's "Battle of Gettysburg" site). They often feature both subject directories and keyword searches.

Specialized databases, which usually search a targeted topic or aspect of a topic, are sometimes hard to find with search engines, but there are websites that specialize in collecting links to them. All three of these types of searching tools are explained in greater detail later in this chapter.

The two most popular organizers of Web content are probably Yahoo! (www.yahoo.com) and Google (www.google.com). Google is known mainly for its search engine, admired by many for the way it produces highly relevant results. Google does offer other services (discussion forums, a subject directory, and news sources) and is regularly adding new ones. Yahoo!, which is older, is known more as a Web **portal**, or a site that offers a range of resources and services, including e-mail, on-line shopping, games, and chat forums. As an information resource, Yahoo! was once identified with its subject directory, in contrast to Google's search engine. But in recent years, Yahoo! has added a search engine. In 2002, Yahoo!'s search engine--and others--began using Google's database in response to Google's popularity, as well as to criticism that Yahoo! search results could be influenced by advertisers who paid for inclusion in its database. Both Google and Yahoo! now accept commercial listings, but they are identified as "sponsored links" or "sponsored matches" and grouped separately, usually at the top of the first results page. Use caution when considering using any information from a site seeking to sell a product (see "Evaluating Online Sources," later in this chapter).

Subject Directories

For general, research-oriented queries, for browsing, and to view sites recommended by experts, use a subject directory. There are two basic types: academic and professional directories, which are most useful to researchers, and commercial portals that cater to the general public.

Here are some commercial portals:

- **About.com**   www.about.com
- **Go.network**   www.go.com
- **Lycos**   www.lycos.com
- **Yahoo!**   www.yahoo.com

For example, in early 2003, Yahoo!'s homepage featured 14 major categories as links to further information. Clicking on "Health" would take you to another page, with dozens more subcategories. Clicking on the subcategory "Teen Health" resulted in links to 60 websites on the subject. They ranged from a government site aimed at helping girls become "fit for life" to a men's magazine site that emphasized selling products as much as offering advice. Yahoo! and other commercial sites do not evaluate user-submitted content when adding Web pages to a database; they leave the evaluation up to the user.

Academic directories, on the other hand, are often annotated by experts and are usually the result of much thought and care. To get started on finding such directories, try the University of Albany list of Internet Subject Directories (http://library.albany.edu/internet/subject.html). Other suggestions:

- **The Librarians' Index to the Internet** (www.lii.org). Sometimes called "the thinking person's Yahoo!."
- **The WWW Virtual Library** (www.vlib.org). One of the oldest and most respected subject directories on the Web. Many of the individual subject collections are maintained at universities.
- **INFOMINE** (infomine.ucr.edu). Compiled by the University of California at Riverside.

Search Engines

For targeted and complex queries, use a search engine. A search engine does not search the entire Internet; it searches **databases,** or collections of logically-related information, that are developed by the company hosting the search engine. That's why different search engines will produce different results. There are at least two ways for a page to be recorded in the search engine's database: the page's publisher can register it with the engine, or the search engine can use software called "spiders" to search the Internet and gather information that is then recorded in the engine's database.

Search engines may offer both subject directories and keyword searches. With most search engines, you enter your search terms and click on a "go" button or hit your return key. Then the engine generates a page with links to resources containing all or some of your terms. The resources are usually ranked by term: that is, one will rank higher if your search term appears many times, near the beginning of the document, in the title, and so forth.

A fairly recent development is a "second-generation" search engine, such as Google, which ranks Web pages according to the number of pages that link to them. This strategy adds an element of human judgment---in essence, it ranks a site by how popular it is--to computer technology. Many users start with Google, even for general queries, because it does such an excellent job of finding relevant documents.

Some popular search engines are:

- **AltaVista**   altavista.digital.com/
- **Excite**   www.excite.com
- **Google**   www.google.com/
- **Hotbot**   www.hotbot.com
- **Webcrawler**   www.webcrawler.com

Your choice of keywords to launch the search is just as important as your choice of search engine. Use the words you would like to find in the title, description, or text of an Internet site. Searching for a common or general word, such as "Clinton," will provide a massive search of every document that contains this term. (The lowercase **clinton** will find both upper- and lower-case instances of

7

the term.) In fact, **clinton** generated 6.9 million results from Google, ranging from Hillary Clinton's official Senate Web page, to a biography of President Clinton, to a Clinton County, Mich., government site--all on the first results page. You'll get more usable results by narrowing your query. Do you want a biography of President Clinton? Clinton's stand on a particular issue? A chronology of Clinton's impeachment trial? Using more than one keyword will narrow your results and make them more relevant to your needs; even with thousands of results, most search engines will put the most relevant pages at the top of the results list.

It's also possible to conduct too narrow a search. If you combine keywords for something like "Ulysses S. Grant's military strategy at Gettysburg," you may produce few or no results. Try dropping one or more keywords until you get a usable list of links.

A **metasearch engine**, instead of creating its own database of information, searches the databases of several search engines. For example, when you enter a query at the Mamma.com website, the engine simultaneously queries about ten of the major search engines, such as Yahoo!, Webcrawler, and Magellan. It then provides you with a short, relevant list of results. **President Clinton impeachment** generated 62 results from Mamma.com, from search engines Teoma, Ask Jeeves, MSN.com, and others. Results included primary sources such as government documents and secondary sources such as press coverage--a mixture that might be useful in writing a college paper.

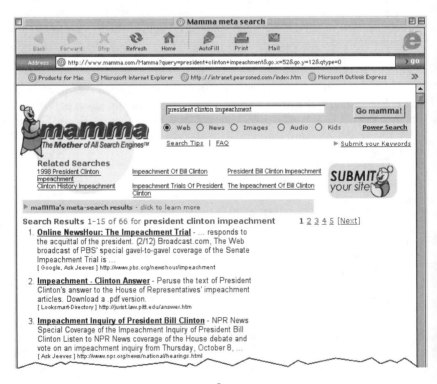

Ixquick is particularly helpful if your topic is obscure or if you want to retrieve results from several search engines without generating an enormous list. Ixquick returns only the top ten relevancy-ranked results from the source search services.

Some popular metasearch engines:

- **Ixquick**   www.ixquick.com
- **ProFusion**   www.profusion.com
- **Dogpile**   www.dogpile.com
- **Mamma.com**   www.mamma.com
- **Metacrawler.com** www.metacrawler.com

Using Boolean Terms
and Other Search Limiters

When you use a search engine, you increase your chances of getting good results by formulating a precise query. Sometimes one word (or keyword) is sufficient, if it is distinctive enough.

Many times you can click on an advanced search option that will bring up a template to prompt you through the process. But sometimes it is helpful to know Boolean logic in order to narrow your search for manageable results.

Boolean logic comes from the ideas of British mathematician George Boole (1815-1864). From his writings come the Boolean operators: AND, OR, and NOT, used to link words and phrases for more precise queries for search engines and directories.

Increasingly, search engines are simplifying their search protocols by making "and" the default logic. If you type **president clinton impeachment** in most search engines, you will get results for the equivalent of **president** AND **clinton** AND **impeachment**.

Be sure to capitalize Boolean operators; some, but not all, search engines, will assume lowercase "and" or "or" to be part of a phrase and consider them "stop" words to be ignored. (Stop words are prepositions, articles, conjunctions, and other common words like **I, an, the, for**.) Most sites offer a link to a page that explains their defaults and other search protocols. From Google's homepage, for example, click on "Advanced Search" and then "Advanced Search Tips" to find this page:

9

Address ⊚ http://www.google.com/help/refinesearch.html   ▶ go

⊚ Products for Mac   ⊚ Microsoft Internet Explorer   ⊚ http://intranet.pearsoned.com/index.htm   ⊚ Microsoft Outlook Express   »

Google™   Advanced Search

Home

All About Google

Help Central

Search Help
Basics of Search
▸ Advanced Search
Interpret Results
Customize

Google Features

General FAQ

Contact Us

Find on this site:

[Search]

Advanced Search Made Easy

You can increase the accuracy of your searches by adding operators that fine-tune your keywords. Most of the options listed on this page can be entered directly into the Google search box or selected from Google's Advanced Search page.

Additionally, Google supports several **advanced operators** which are query words that have special meaning to Google. For a complete list, click here.

" + " Searches

Google ignores common words and characters such as "where" and "how", as well as certain single digits and single letters, because they tend to slow down your search without improving the results. Google will indicate if a common word has been excluded by displaying details on the results page below the search box.

If a common word is essential to getting the results you want, you can include it by putting a "+" sign in front of it. (Be sure to include a space before the "+" sign.)

Another method for doing this is conducting a phrase search, which simply means putting quotation marks around 2 or more words. Common words in a phrase search (e.g., "where are you") are included in the search.

For example, to search for Star Wars, Episode I, use:

Star Wars Episode +I   [**Google Search**]

" - " Searches

Boolean AND, OR, and NOT

The Boolean AND narrows your search by retrieving only documents that contain every one of the keywords you enter. The more terms you enter, the narrower your search becomes. Examples:

- gene AND therapy
- gene AND therapy AND risks

An Altavista search of **gene AND therapy** turned up more than 339,000 results; **gene AND therapy AND risks** generated 48,000.

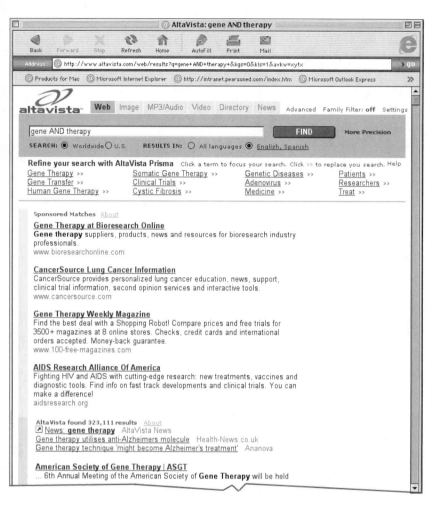

The Boolean OR expands your search by returning documents in which either or both keywords appear. Since the OR operator is usually used for keywords that are similar or synonymous, the more keywords you enter, the more documents you will retrieve. If you do a Google search of two keywords using OR and AND, you will see how OR broadens your search while AND narrows it:

- sea lions OR walruses (192,000 results)
- sea lions AND walruses (6,250 results)

The Boolean NOT or AND NOT limits your search by returning documents with only your first keyword but not the second, even if the first word appears in that document, too. For example, if you type in **seals** as a keyword, you'll get many results about Easter Seals. But if you wanted information on the animal, you could type:

- seals NOT Easter
- seals AND NOT Easter

Many search engines convert formal Boolean operators into more user-friendly template terminology when you enter their advanced search pages. The Google advanced search template gives you these options:

In the template above, "all the words" is equivalent to the Boolean AND; "at least one of the words," the Boolean OR; and "without the words," the Boolean NOT. "Exact phrase" means that if you type in **President Clinton,** you will get pages where **Clinton** is always preceded by **President**; if you use the "all the words" option and type **President Clinton**, you'll get pages with **President** and **Clinton**, but not necessarily together as a phrase.

Implied and Other Non-Boolean Limiters

While full Boolean operators are accepted in the advanced search option of some search engines, "implied" Boolean operators--or what some call "search engine math"--are accepted in the basic search options of an increasing number of search engines.

Implied Boolean operators use the plus (+) symbol for AND:

- gene +therapy +risks

The implied Boolean operator for NOT is a minus (-) symbol. Typing a (+) or (-) sign in front of a word will force the inclusion or exclusion of that word in the search statement.

- pinnipeds -walruses
- Star Wars Episode +I

Search engines have different rules about spacing before and after plus or minus signs. Google specifies a space before the symbol and no space after.

The "plus" technique is helpful when a key part of your search term is normally a stop word that a search engine would ignore. For example, typing **Star Wars Episode I** into Google will return results about all Star Wars episodes because Google will eliminate the "I" as a common word. Adding "+I" will return results only about Episode I.

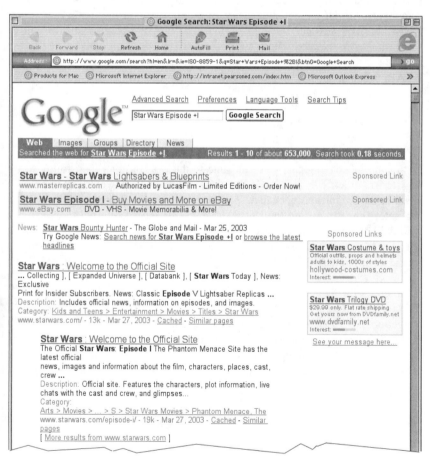

Implied Boolean operators have no symbol for OR. A few search engines default to OR when two terms are searched (**war battle**), but most default to AND.

Quotation Marks

In most search engines, you can use quotation marks around two or more words to make them one unit (although proper names usually do not need quotation marks).

- "gene therapy risks"
- "SUV gas mileage"

Other Limiters

Proximity, or positional, operators--ADJ, for adjacent, or NEAR--are not really part of Boolean logic, but they serve a similar function in formulating search statements. Not all search engines accept proximity operators, but a few accept NEAR in their advanced search option. The NEAR operator allows you to search for terms situated within a specified distance of each other in any order. The closer they are, the higher the document appears in the results list. Using NEAR, when possible, in place of the Boolean AND usually returns more relevant results.

- sea lions NEAR pinnipeds
- Cheney NEAR Bush

With some search engines, you can truncate the word: use its root, followed by an asterisk, to retrieve variants of the word. For example, if you can't remember whether the organization is called Feminine Majority or Feminist Majority, you can enter **femini*** to find the site you want. This is also referred to as using a wild card or "stemming." Yahoo! supports wild card searches, but Google does not; if you don't get the results you want with one form of the word in Google, try the other (**walrus OR walruses**).

Another useful technique with some search engines is **field limiting,** which limits searches to a specified part of a page: title, URL, link, host, domain, image, or text, for example. Type in the field followed by a colon. If you wanted to make sure "multiple sclerosis" was in the title of a page in order to call up only sites devoted to the topic, you'd search for **title: multiple sclerosis**. Google uses "allintitle" for a title search, so a search for **allintitle: multiple sclerosis** would yield these results:

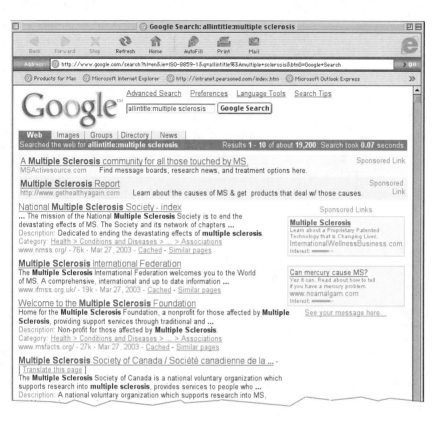

Online Databases

Much of the World Wide Web is not directly searchable from most search engines--the information is so specialized or constantly changing that it is "invisible" to the software that search engines use to access databases. These databases are often referred to as the "invisible Web" or "deep Web." Yet information stored in these databases is accessible if you know how to find it.

Some search engines and portals help by offering separate search options for the kinds of dynamically changing information, such as job listings and news, that search engines normally can't find. Yahoo's HotJobs (hotjobs.yahoo.com) and Google's news site (news.google.com) are examples of specialized search functions separate from the company's main search engine. Some sites also offer search options for multimedia and image files (Google's Image Search), and files created in non-standard file types such as Portable Document Format (PDF).

There are websites that specialize in collecting links to databases available on the Web. One such site is called The Invisible Web (www.invisibleweb.com) and links to 10,000 Web-accessible databases.

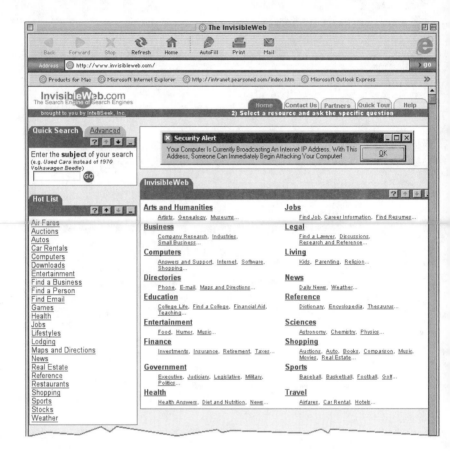

You may also want to visit other sites that collect links to Web databases:

- **Resource Discovery Network**   www.rdn.ac.uk
- **ProFusion**   www.profusion.com
- **Complete Planet**   www.completeplanet.com
- **Geniusfind**   geniusfind.com

Strategies for Searching Online Databases

Google and other search engines can locate searchable databases by searching a subject term and the word "database." For example, type **aviation accidents database** in Google, and you will get thousands of results, including a federal government database with information from 1962 and later about civil aviation accidents in the United States.

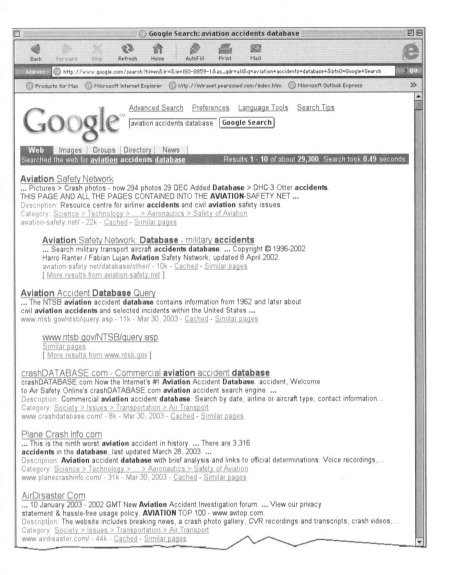

The word **database** is also helpful in searching a topic in Yahoo!, because Yahoo! uses the term to describe searchable databases in its listings. Examples:

- U.S. presidential election results database
- languages database
- toxic chemicals database

Such databases, especially if they are sponsored by government sites (identified by the **.gov** at the end of the URL), can be extremely useful as primary sources.

Planning a Search Strategy

The University of California at Berkeley has come up with a checklist (http://www.lib.berkeley.edu/TeachingLib/Guides/Internet/Strategies.html) to help you plan your search strategy. The first step is to analyze your topic to decide where to begin. Then you pick the right starting point depending on your analysis:

- If it has a distinctive word or phrase ("Battle of Gettysburg"), enclose the phrase in double quotation marks and test-run it in Google. Or search the broader concept in a subject directory.

- If it has *no* distinctive words or phrases, use more than one term or a phrase in double quotes to get fewer results from a search engine. Or try to find distinctive terms in subject directories.

- If you want an overview ("energy conservation"), look for a specialized subject directory on your topic.

- If you're seeking a narrow aspect of a broad or common topic (the role of governors in death-row pardons), try AltaVista's advanced search (www.altavista.com) or look for a directory focused on the broad subject (capital punishment).

- If your topic has synonyms (sea lion or pinniped), equivalent terms (energy conservation or fuel conservation), variant spellings (Thelonious Monk or Thelonius Monk), or endings that need to be included, choose engines with Boolean logic or truncation.

- If you don't even know where to start--you're confused and need more information--look for a gateway page or subject guide (Research Navigator's Link Library, www.researchnavigator.com), try an encyclopedia in a virtual library (the Internet Public Library, www.ipl.org), or ask at a library reference desk.

Then, stay flexible: learn as you go and vary your approach with what you learn. Don't get bogged down in a strategy that doesn't work. Switch from search engines to directories and vice versa. Find specialized directories on your topic and possible databases.

Evaluating Online Sources

In your career as a student and eventually as a professional, you will spend a great deal of time using the Internet to communicate and find information. But can you trust the information you find?

Suppose you come across two arguments regarding the greenhouse gas effect and global warming. Here are the views of a scientist who believes there is little or no greenhouse gas effect:

> Although thermometers located at Earth's surface indicate that the planet's average temperature is higher today by about 1°F than it was 140 years ago, satellite measurements of the temperature of the atmosphere thousands of feet above the surface indicate little or no warming since 1979. The difference between temperatures aloft and at the surface is not predicted by computer climate models. Therefore these models cannot be relied upon to project future warming, and the surface warming itself may be an artifact caused by urban heat islands rather than a true global warming trend.

Here is the response of an environmental organization that believes global warming is human-caused and a real threat to the environment:

> The method of translation of the satellite data into temperatures has been revised several times as errors were found and it is still not clear that these data provide a reliable means to determine long term trends. At higher altitudes, temperatures fluctuate more than at the surface due to natural climate influences like sunlight-reflecting particles from volcanoes. This variability or noise in the satellite record obscures the warming trend due to the buildup of the greenhouse gases, which is apparent in the global surface temperature data.

Which is more credible, the dissident scientist or the environmental organization? The organization also cites scientific research to back up its arguments. Because experts disagree, we need to consider the source.

Criteria for Evaluating Online Sources

How do you know which authorities and online sources to trust? When you look for information, you need to know the basis of the author's authority. Here are some questions you can ask to answer the question: How dependable is the source?

- Is the authority well-known and well-regarded?

- What are the authority's credentials (position, institutional affiliation)? You can check the Web page for a biography, check links to other documents, or check the author's homepage.

- Was the authority in a position to have access to pertinent facts? Someone who was a firsthand observer of the events in question is usually (but not always) more reliable. In general, primary sources are more impressive than secondary sources.

- Has the authority been screened by some organization? For example, articles in academic journals are evaluated by peers--experts in the field--to help determine if they should be accepted for publication.

- What are the likely biases? Factors that can influence how evidence is reported are personal needs, prior expectations, general beliefs, attitudes, values, theories, and ideologies. Few experts are without bias, but some have less bias than others. We can try to determine that bias by seeking information about the authority's personal interest in the topic of discussion. We need to be especially wary if an authority stands to benefit financially from the actions he or she advocates.

- How scholarly and fair has the author been? Does the author show knowledge of related sources, with appropriate citations? If claims need empirical support, does the author provide research evidence? If the topic is controversial, does the author acknowledge this and present several sides of the issue, or is the presentation one-sided? Does the document include a full biography, with references to high-quality sources, including primary sources and recent scholarly reviews? Is the information recent and up-to- date?

- Is the information timely and up-to-date? When was it produced and last updated?

Differences Among Sources of Information on the Web

The motives and purposes of those who put up websites vary greatly, and those differences affect the quality of the information. To determine the likely motives of website sponsors, you need to know who the sponsors are. Try to determine the following about any site you are using for information:

- The name of the organization or individual responsible.
- Links to additional information about the organization or individual.
- A clear statement of the site's goals.
- A clear indication of any financial sponsors and whether they are profit or nonprofit.

Your next question is: What are the likely motives of the source? Some possibilities:

- **To inform.** Many websites exist simply to present information on a topic. URL addresses that end in **.edu** or **.gov** tend to be informational because they are sponsored by educational institutions or by government agencies. Some examples: Library of Congress (lcweb.loc.gov), U.S. Environmental Protection Agency (www.epa.gov), the Internet Encyclopedia of Philosophy (www.utm.edu/research/iep/) and the U.S. Department of Commerce (www.commerce.gov).

- **To advocate.** The purpose of an advocacy page is to persuade you. Such pages reflect strong biases, which you need to identify in judging the quality of the information. URL addresses often end in **.org** if they are sponsored by a nonprofit organization. If a site's authors and sponsors seek financial donations, promote a cause, try to recruit members to an organization or provide ways for like-mind people to pursue further contact, it is an advocacy page. Organizations like Planned Parenthood, the National Rifle Association, the National Organization for Women, the Christian Coalition, and the ACLU sponsor advocacy sites.

- **To sell.** The primary purpose of many websites is to promote or sell products or services; you need to be especially alert to biases in information from such sites. URL addresses whose purpose is to sell often end in **.com**. Examples: Amazon.com, Ebay, the Gap, and Circuit City.

- **To provide news.** Many of these sites are postings of news from traditional print sources such as *The New York Times*, *USA Today*, *Newsweek*, and *Time*. Some news sites (Slate.com and Salon.com, for example) gather information from and link to multiple news sites as well as providing their own content.

- **To express individual opinions**. Many websites are created by individuals who want to express themselves. They may take the form of online journals, art galleries, or poetry sites. Web logs, called "blogs," whose authors comment on issues and link to news sites or like-minded Web authors, are increasingly popular. Personal opinion Web pages are very diverse and often very biased. Find out as much as you can about the person behind the site to decide how much credence to give his or her opinions.

- **Mixed motives.** Websites often reflect multiple motives. Be especially alert to sites that suggest one motive (information) but actually reflect other important motives (such as selling). An example is the "teen health" site listed on Yahoo! that is sponsored by a men's magazine--it blankets the site with advertising for health products. Another common practice is to make a website look as though it is informing when it is also advocating. If you are writing a paper on gun control, you may want to review sites sponsored by both pro- and anti-gun groups, but keep in mind their biases before you use any information from them.

Omitted Information

The information that you find at any particular site is selective. There are limitations imposed by time and space. Readers have limited attention spans and the communicator's knowledge is always incomplete. Sometimes, an author means to deceive: advertisers omit information that reflects badly on their products, and experts sometimes leave out information that would weaken their arguments. Finally, people have different values, beliefs, and attitudes. An individual's perspective may prevent him from noting information presented by those with different perspectives.

To get a fair picture of an issue or make a sound judgment on a research question, you need to pursue the omitted information. As you read a document, ask yourself questions to help you fill in what is missing:

- **Counterarguments**. What reasons would someone who disagrees offer? Are there research studies that contradict the studies presented? Are there missing examples that support the other side of the argument?

- **Definitions**. How would the arguments differ if key terms were defined in other ways?

- **Value preferences or perspectives**. From what other set of values might one approach this issue?

- **Origins of "facts" alluded to in the argument**. Are the factual claims supported by well-done research or by reliable sources?

- **Process used for gathering facts**. Was a survey conducted scientifically? How were respondents chosen and how were questions worded?

- **Figures, graphs, and data**. Would statistical results look different if they included evidence from different years? Have figures been selected to make a stronger case?

- **Effects of what is advocated or opposed**. What are the proposal's impacts, positive and negative, short- and long-term? Could there be unintended consequences? Which segments of society would gain and which would lose? What about other impacts: political, economic, biological, spiritual, health, interpersonal, or environmental?

- **Benefits accruing to the author.** Will the author benefit financially if we adopt his or her proposal?

Of course, reasoning is always incomplete. You could never form an opinion if you believed you had to find every possible piece of information on the subject first. But you can improve your arguments and your writing by gathering the most reliable and current information possible, given your limitations of time and space.

Chapter 3

Avoiding Plagiarism and Using Sources Ethically

What Is Plagiarism?

It is plagiarism to present another person's words or ideas as if they were your own. A kind of theft, plagarism can result in failing a course or even in expulsion from college. While blatant, intentional plagiarism is not the campus norm, many students fail to fully understand what constitutes plagiarism. Internet research in particular poses pitfalls: information can be copied from the Web with the click of a mouse, and too many students wrongly believe that anything on the Internet is in the public domain (see the section "Using Copyrighted Materials" at the end of this chapter). Others believe that they can escape detection because a professor couldn't read all the possible sources on a topic; however, instructors can now access websites that scan documents and search the Internet to identify plagiarized material.

The most flagrant forms of plagiarism are the use of another student's work, the purchase of a "canned" research paper, or knowingly copying passages into a research paper without documentation. Sometimes students unintentionally plagiarize through carelessness--by leaving off quotation marks or failing to document sources properly. Also, too many students believe that merely changing sentence order or a few words in a passage avoids plagiarism.

How to Avoid Plagiarism

Always credit the source for any ideas and words not your own. That said, a fear of plagiarism should not force you to document the obvious. You do not have to document common knowledge--information that most educated people know. (For example, that George W. Bush did not win the popular vote in the 2000 presidential election is common knowledge; a newspaper citation would be unnecessary.) You also do not have to document your own thinking, including points or conclusions that you have reached through the course of your research.

Paraphrasing

When you paraphrase, you restate *in your own words* a passage written or spoken by another person--and no more. Your writing should reflect the original passage's emphasis in your own phrasing and sentence structure. Compare the following passages. Here's the original, from a Stanford University website on South Africa:

> With the enactment of apartheid laws in 1948, racial discrimination was institutionalized. Race laws touched every aspect of social life, including a prohibition of marriage between non-whites and whites, and the sanctioning of "white-only" jobs. In 1950, the Population Registration Act required that all South Africans be racially classified into one of three categories, white, black (African) or colored (of mixed descent). The colored category included major subgroups of Indians and Asians. Classification into these categories was based on appearance, social acceptance and descent. For example, a white person was defined as "in appearance obviously a white person or generally accepted as a white person." A person could not be considered white if one of his or her parents were non-white. The determination that a person was "obviously white" would take into account "his habits, education and speech, and deportment and demeanor" (Chokshi, Carter, Gupta, Martin, & Allen, 1991).

Unacceptable Paraphrase (underlined words are plagiarized):

> According to Chokshi et al. (1991), racial discrimination was institutionalized with passage of the apartheid laws in 1948. Race laws touched every aspect of social life, including banning marriage between races, and the sanctioning of "white-only" jobs. The 1950 Population Registration Act required that all South Africans be racially classified as white, black (African) or colored (of mixed descent, Indian or Asian). Classification was based on appearance, social acceptance and descent. A white person, for example, was "in appearance obviously a white person or generally accepted as a white person." A person could not be considered white if one of his parents were non-white. According to the act, determining that a person was "obviously white" would take into account "his habits, education and speech, and deportment and demeanor.

In the above example, citing the authors (Chokshi et al., meaning "Chokshi and others") at the beginning does not legitimize using the authors' exact wording-- nor does changing a few words and the order of phrases.

Acceptable Paraphrase:

> The 1948 apartheid laws made racial discrimination official. The wide-ranging laws allowed "white-only" jobs and banned marriage between races. Two years later, the Population Registration Act classified all South Africans into one of three racial categories: white, black

(African) or colored. "Colored" South Africans were of mixed descent or were Indians or Asians. According to Chokshi et al. (1991), the categories were determined by "appearance, social acceptance and descent." An officially "white" person, then, had been judged to look like a white person or was accepted as one. A white person could not have a non-white parent. The act posited that "habits, education and speech, and deportment and demeanor" would help determine the classification.

Here, the writer has borrowed two phrases from the original, but enclosed them in quotes or attributed them properly--to Chokshi et al. and the Population Registration Act.

Summarizing

A summary condenses the essentials of someone else's thought into a few statements. A summary is shorter than a paraphrase and provides only the main point from the original source. Keep it short; a summary should reduce the original by at least half. As with a paraphrase, keep your own ideas and opinions separate; you may want to note them to yourself and use them elsewhere in your paper, however.

Here is how the above quotation could be summarized:

The 1948 apartheid laws institutionalized racial discrimination in South Africa, affecting all aspects of social life. The 1950 Population Registration Act set up three categories of races, determined by such factors as appearance and descent (Chokshi, Carter, Gupta, Martin & Allen, 1991).

How to Include Reference Citations in Your Text

As you take notes, keep meticulous track of your sources. You may want to print a hard copy of each Web article used in order to save the author or authors, organization, title, date and URL for later reference--especially since Web pages are created and taken down constantly. Find out which documentation standard your instructor is using. The major styles used are MLA (Modern Language Association), APA (American Psychological Association), CMS (Chicago Manual of Style), or CBE (Council of Biology Editors, now the Council of Science Editors). All of these styles may be found on the Research Navigator homepage (www.researchnavigator.com) at the "Citing Your Sources" tab.

Here's how the entry on your "Works Cited" page would look for the apartheid quote using APA style:

Monal Chokshi, Cale Carter, Deepak Gupta, Tove Martin & Robert Allen (1991). Computers and the apartheid regime in South Africa. *South Africa. Guide to Internet Resources. Stanford University.* Retrieved Dec. 12, 2002, from the World Wide Web: http://www-cs-students.stanford.edu/~cale/cs201

In the example above, the authors' names are followed by the year the paper was written, the paper's title, and the name of the website (in italics). The date it was retrieved is followed by the URL. If the source is from a journal, you'll need to include the title of the periodical or electronic text, volume number, and pages.

The process for citing a Web source within text is similar to citing a print source. Within your text, you will need to provide enough information to identify a source with a name or website. If the site includes page numbers or paragraph numbers, use those as well. (In subsequent references to the same authority, the author's last name is usually sufficient.) Keep citations brief; you will fully document each source on the "Works Cited" page. If no author is listed, use the article title or website information for your in-text citation:

> South Africa's minority government used technology--especially computer hardware and software--as a tool of repression (*Computers and the Apartheid Regime in South Africa*, 1991).

Quoting Sources

Direct quotations from online material follow the same rules as non-Internet material. Enclose within quotations marks all quoted materials--a phrase, a sentence, a paragraph. (Some documentation styles specify that if you are quoting more than a sentence or two, the quote should be indented instead and set off typographically.)

Don't load a paper with quotations; if more than a quarter of your essay consists of quotations, you are letting others speak for you and giving the impression that you have not synthesized the material. When drawing from an authority, rely mostly on paraphrase and summary. *Do* use a quotation, however, when it fits your message and its language is particularly on point or if the idea is hard to paraphrase accurately.

> Diane Sollee (1996), the founder and director of the Coalition for Marriage, Family and Couples Education, said, "The number one predictor of divorce is the habitual avoidance of conflict."

Quote exactly; if you drop a quoted phrase within a sentence, make sure the grammar meshes with your own. If you eliminate a sentence or words within the quote, use ellipses according to the appropriate documentation style.

Halberstam (2001) described "… a dramatically changed America, one which has been challenged by the cruelest kind of terrorism, and which is in a kind of suspended state between war and peace …and where so much of our normal agenda has been brushed aside."

Using Copyrighted Materials

Just as a patent protects an inventor's rights to exploit a new product, a copyright signifies original creation and ownership of written words, music, or images. As a student, you may use copyrighted material in your research paper under the doctrine of fair use, which allows the use of others' words for such informational purposes as criticism, comment, news reporting, teaching, scholarship, or research. Academic integrity requires documenting such use in the manner covered in this chapter.

Copyright law is not intended to halt the flow of ideas and facts; it is meant to protect the literary, musical, or visual form that an author or artist uses to express his concepts. For example, there is a popular poem called "Warning" by Jenny Joseph (1961) that begins, "When I am an old woman I shall wear purple/ With a red hat which doesn't go and doesn't suit me." Several websites publish a shorter, adapted version of the poem, but anyone who wants a full version is directed to buy products from a company that has bought publishing rights to the poem. If anyone could sell products displaying Joseph's poem, its value to Joseph and the authorized publisher would be greatly diminished. Few artworks are as commercial as this, but a literary critic who published, without permission, all seven lines of a seven-line poem in her review would be violating copyright law as well. In either case, it *is* permissible to describe the ideas and facts contained in a work or quote brief passages; what is *not* permissible is to copy or reprint large portions of the work in its original literary, musical, or visual format without permission.

If you use substantial blocks of material, or you want to download images for your paper, you should seek permission from the author or website. When in doubt, consult your instructor or e-mail the author or another contact for the Internet site.

Chapter 4

Introducing Research Navigator™

What Is Research Navigator and How Can It Help with Research?

Research Navigator is an online academic research service that combines three major databases with practical research assistance--all in one place on the Web. It can help you understand the steps in the research process while also providing in-depth information on conducting library research.

Research Navigator offers these databases of credible and reliable source material: EBSCO's ContentSelect Academic Journal and Abstract Database, The *New York Times* Search by Subject Archive, and "Best of the Web" Link Library. It also guides students step-by-step through the writing of a research paper. Access to Research Navigator is free with the purchase of any Pearson Education college textbook.

To begin using Research Navigator, register with the personal access code found in this *Guide to Online Research.* Once you register, you have access to all the resources in Research Navigator for six months.

What's in Research Navigator?

From the homepage, you can gain access to all of the site's main features, including the three databases--for academic journals and general interest publications (EBSCO's ContentSelect), newspaper articles (The *New York Times* Search by Subject Archive), and World Wide Web sites ("Best of the Web" Link Library)--that will be discussed in greater detail later. If you are new to the research process, you may want to start by browsing "Understanding the Research Process," located in the upper right-hand section of the homepage. Here you will find help on all aspects of conducting research, from gathering data to searching the Internet, evaluating sources, drafting the paper, and revising and editing the final draft.

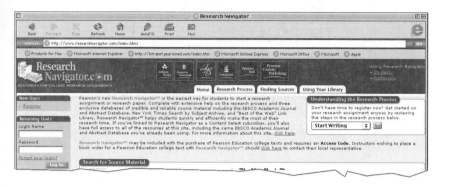

ContentSelect

EBSCO's ContentSelect Research Database gives you instant access to thousands of academic journals and periodicals from any computer with an Internet connection.

When you need the most authoritative take on a subject, especially one that is complex or very specialized, you will turn to academic journals. Academic journals are aimed at a professional audience--researchers, instructors, and experts, usually affiliated with colleges and universities. Academic-journal articles have been peer-reviewed before publication; that is, they have been checked for balance, methodology, and significance by other experts in the field. An article that doesn't meet the profession's standards will not be published in an academic journal. Examples of academic journals are *Science, Nature, American Ethnologist, Journal of Chemical Education*, and *Canadian Journal of Sociology.*

When you do a search, your list will include some results in full-text format. The full article may be in HTML, the common language used to write Web documents, or it may be in a PDF format. PDF is a file format that creates high-resolution documents; to read such documents, however, you need to first download a free viewer, Adobe Acrobat Reader.

Many ContentSelect results will be in a citation format; when you click on those results, you will get a bibliographic reference with author, subject, and journal source. A citation will usually contain an abstract, or brief summary of the article, that will help you determine whether you want to find the full article. You then find the full article through the journal's online archive, or in a print or electronic version through your college library's catalog.

To use ContentSelect, select a database to search and then enter a keyword. For more detailed information, see Chapter 7.

The *New York Times*
Search by Subject Archive

Among daily newspapers, the *New York Times* is the gold standard. It is widely considered the nation's newspaper of record because it is comprehensive and staffed by reporters and editors who are experienced and well-regarded. It has substantial resources and a tradition of excellence.

The *Times*, however, like other newspapers, is aimed at a general audience and is limited by daily deadlines, competitive pressures, and space, so individual articles may not be suitable sources for a complex or very specialized research topic. But for day-to-day coverage of events and popular issues, and general, accessible background information on a wide range of topics, it is first rate.

Research Navigator gives you access to a one-year archive of articles from the *New York Times*. The archives are searchable by subject and by keyword. For tips on how to use the *New York Times* archive, see Chapter 5. Articles can be printed or saved for later use in your research assignment. Be sure to review the rules for citing a newspaper article in endnotes or a bibliography.

Link Library

Link Library is a collection of links to websites, organized by academic subject and key terms. To use this database, select a subject from the drop-down list. You will be taken to a list of key terms; find the key term for your subject and see a list of five or more editorially reviewed websites that offer educationally relevant and credible content. The Web links in Link Library are monitored and updated each week, reducing your chances of encountering dead links.

Other Resources within Research Navigator

Using Your Library

Despite the Internet revolution, a visit to a bricks-and-mortar library continues to be an important part of the research process. Use the drop-down list on the

Research Navigator homepage "Using Your Library" tab to select a "Library Guide" for your subject. The guide will list Library of Congress and Dewey call numbers, major print and online journals, organizations and associations, discussion lists, and Internet resources. Print it out and take it with you to help you navigate a library's vast resources more efficiently.

"Using Your Library" also discusses types of libraries, their resources, how to choose which ones to use, and the research process and how to develop a timeframe for it.

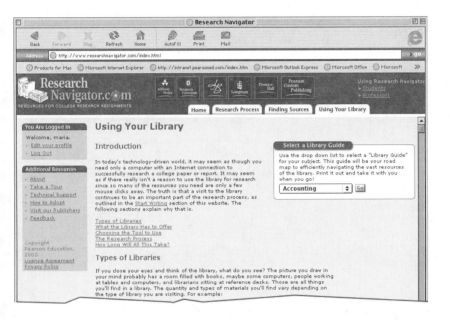

The Research Process

There are several key steps to the research process, beginning with the selection of a research topic and the development of a tentative thesis. The three hyperlinked sections under the "Research Process" tab--"Start Writing," "Internet Research," and "Citing Sources"--explain the research process in greater detail, including how to evaluate good source material, how to properly cite sources, and how to develop endnotes or a bibliography.

Screenshot of the Research Navigator website showing the Research Process page.

Within the browser window:

Research Navigator.com
RESOURCES FOR COLLEGE RESEARCH ASSIGNMENTS

Home | Research Process | Finding Sources | Using Your Library

Using Research Navigator
▸ Students
▸ Professors

You Are Logged In
Welcome, maria.
▸ Edit your profile
▸ Log Out

Additional Resources
▸ About
▸ Take a Tour
▸ Technical Support
▸ How to Adopt
▸ Visit our Publishers
▸ Feedback

Copyright
Pearson Education,
2002.
License Agreement
Privacy Policy

Research Process

Understanding the research process is important to your success in college. It is applied to research papers and reports, as well as some class projects, labs, and even homework assignments. There are several key steps involved in the process, beginning with the selection of a research topic and the development of a tentative thesis, which is the argument that you will be defending in your research paper. Idea-generating methods for identifying a research topic may include brainstorming, reading through books or journal articles, or discussions with peers or instructors.

After you've decided on a research topic, you can set out to find sources of supporting information. Such sources may include -- but are not limited to -- books, journal articles, newspapers, web sites, interviews, etc. Be sure to take notes, a step that will later help in organizing material and properly documenting sources.

The next main step in the research process involves the actual writing of the paper, report, or project. Working from your notes, you summarize, paraphrase, and incorporate direct quotes into a draft. This draft can undergo one or more content revisions before a final draft is completed. Next, it is essential that you "give credit" to your sources through endnotes, footnotes, a bibliography, or just simply a list of sources. As a final step, the written document should always be edited prior to submission.

Below are three hyperlinked sections that explain the research process in greater detail – including how to evaluate good source material, how to properly cite your sources, and how to develop endnotes or a bibliography. Working through these steps will quickly put you on the right track to completing your research assignment. Once you've reviewed these sections and have an understanding of your research assignment, click on the Finding Sources tab to begin you search for credible and reliable source material. Then check out the Using Your Library tab to understand how to use library resources effectively and efficiently.

Understanding the Research Process

Don't have time to register now? Get started on your research assignment anyway by reviewing the steps in the research process below.

[Start Writing ▼] [Go]

Finding Sources

This section of Research Navigator helps start your search for credible and reliable source material by offering three databases of source material, similar to those offered by a library. EBSCO's Academic Journal and Abstract Database gives you journal articles from leading academic journals as well as articles from many leading popular periodicals, such as *Newsweek* and *USA Today*. The *New York Times* Search by Subject Archive lets you review newspaper articles from the past year, and Link Library points you to the "Best of the Web" sites that have been screened for educational relevance to key topics.

If you need more source material, or are ready to go to the library to conduct a more detailed and thorough search, click on "Using Your Library" and review suggestions for making the most of your time at the library.

Chapter 5

Using the *New York Times* Search by Subject Archive

About the *New York Times*

Newspapers, also known as periodicals because they are issued in periodic installments (e.g. daily, weekly, or monthly), provide contemporary information. Although they don't have the scholarly authority of academic journals, newspapers are often the best source of the latest information on popular and controversial topics. Political struggles, economic debates, election campaigns and issues, scientific advances, the arts and contemporary social trends are all extensively covered by periodicals.

Research Navigator gives you access to a search-by-subject archive of articles from one of the world's leading newspapers: the *New York Times*. Since its founding in 1851, the *New York Times* has become the nation's newspaper of record--the publication that other media look to as a guide for coverage and responsible news judgment. The *Times* is still the leader among news organizations in winning Pulitzer Prizes, journalism's top award, with 108 prizes through 2002. It employs more than 1,000 editors, reporters, photographers, artists, and designers in its news department. Its reach is truly global: in 2001, the *Times* had 30 reporters in Washington, D.C.; 30 reporters in U.S. bureaus outside Washington and New York; and 40 staff correspondents and contributors in 26 news bureaus around the world.

Using the criteria we established in Chapter 2 for the dependability of sources, the *Times*:

- is well-known and well-regarded.
- has impressive credentials (Pulitzer Prizes, experienced reporters and editors).
- has access to pertinent facts (numerous correspondents provide firsthand accounts worldwide).

On the other hand, *Times* content is not peer-reviewed in the way that an academic journal is. Its content *is* screened informally by media observers and

33

critics who are quick to pounce on any perceived errors or biases. In recent years, questions have been raised about the *Times'* coverage of a cancer "breakthrough," an Asian-American scientist suspected of being a spy, and attendance at anti-Iraq-war rallies. When *Times* editors have been convinced that criticisms have merit, they have published follow-up stories or editor's notes acknowledging errors of fact or emphasis. When smaller factual errors come to light, the *Times*, like most leading newspapers, prints timely corrections; some online archives, such as LexisNexis, append the corrections to the story.

So, while the *Times* is an excellent source for information on current topics, keep in mind that it has daily deadlines, competitive pressures, and fallible editors and reporters--like all newspapers. You need to apply the same skepticism toward the information it provides as you would with any other source. Check factual claims with other sources and be alert for signs of bias and omitted information.

What's in the Archive?

Research Navigator's *New York Times* archive organizes articles published in the past year by more than 135 academic subjects, from accounting to zoology. It only includes articles deemed relevant and timely for research; you will not find recipes or wedding announcements. The *Times* archive contents are updated every day.

The *Times'* regular website, www.nytimes.com, contains the full content of the print edition as well as additional articles and images. The newspaper's own archive includes articles from as far back as January 1, 1996, but at the time this guide was written, the *Times* charged a fee to access articles--except for art, book, and entertainment reviews--that were more than seven days old.

When and How to Use *New York Times* Articles

If you want to know the latest on an issue or breaking news story, check Research Navigator's *New York Times* archive. Want to know the status of congressional action regarding offshore income-tax shelters? What are the most recent developments with charter schools? What are the two political parties' stands on affirmative action? Go to the relevant subject directory, or do a keyword search, or both.

But if you are researching existential philosophers, European colonialism in the Congo, or the photography of Walker Evans, for example, a newspaper archive is not the place to start. For non-contemporary subjects, especially complex academic topics, you should consider academic journals, subject directories, and search engines for finding online sources. Research Navigator's ContentSelect and Link Library, which are explained in the next two chapters, will help you find directories and search engines more suited to your topic.

Searching the Archive

Search by Subject

Searching the *New York Times* archive by subject is not only easy, it's also more suited to browsing than to finding a specific topic. The "constitutional law" grouping had 166 articles when this was written, and the "American government" heading had nearly 4,000. But once you have called up a subject area, you are taken to an advanced search page and you can further refine your search with a keyword or words. Articles can be printed or saved for later use. Be sure to review the citation rules for how to cite a newspaper article in endnotes or a bibliography.

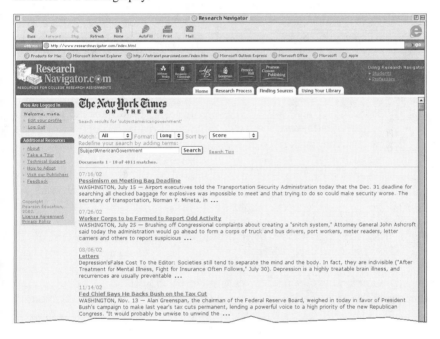

Search by Keyword

Type a word, or multiple words separated by commas, into the search box. If you are using more than one word, there are three **match** options for you to choose from.

- The "All" option will pull up all articles with all of the key terms you enter as well as their various word endings. So, for example, if you search for articles with the words **Enron** and **auditor**, your search results will include articles that contain the words **Enron** and **auditor** as well as articles that contain the words **Enron** and **auditors**.

- The "Any" option is equivalent to the Boolean "or." It will pull up all articles with any of the terms you enter. Using the same key words as above, **Enron** and **auditor**, the "any" option will yield articles that contain the words **Enron** or **auditor** or **auditors**.

- The "Boolean" option lets you use the Boolean operators "and," "or," and "not" to refine your search. See Chapter 2 for more information on using Boolean terms.

In addition, there are two **format** options: "Long" and "Short." The search results for the default, Long, will include headlines and the first five lines from each of the articles. The alternative, Short, will just list the article headlines.

Finally, there are six **sort by** options from which to choose.

- The default, "Score," presents search results in order of the number of times your key words appear in the articles. "Reverse Score" does just the opposite: it lists search results from those articles with the fewest mentions of your key terms first.

- Selecting "Time" will yield results from the most recent to the oldest articles in the archive. Conversely, "Reverse Time" results are presented from oldest to most recent.

- Searching by "Title" will produce articles in alphabetical order based on the first word in the headline. "Reverse Title" will do the opposite.

The most useful of these options are probably the search by "Score," which ranks articles by the number of times they mention your search terms, and "Time" or "Reverse Time," which ranks the articles chronologically.

In the example above, suppose you were researching the role of accounting auditors in the Enron business scandal. At the time this was written, if you used the "Any" option for **Enron** and **auditor**, you'd get 2,708 results, many of them not useful because they included any article from the past year that mentioned "auditor" and any article that included "Enron." If you used the "All" option, you would get 481 results. You could also use the "sort by" options to make the list even more manageable, depending upon whether you wanted the most recent stories (select "Time") or the stories that have more mentions of your terms (select "Score"). If you want to narrow the results yet again, add another keyword. If you searched for **Enron**, **auditor**, and **Andersen** (for the accounting firm), you would get 343 matches. In addition, clicking on the "Long" form will let you read the headline and first paragraph of each article, but using the "Short" form, with headlines only, may help you scan results more quickly.

Back · Forward · Stop · Refresh · Home · AutoFill · Print · Mail

Address: http://www.researchnavigator.com/index.html · go

Products for Mac · Microsoft Internet Explorer · http://intranet.pearsoned.com/index.htm · Microsoft Outlook Express · Microsoft Office · Microsoft · Apple

Research Navigator.c⊛m
RESOURCES FOR COLLEGE RESEARCH ASSIGNMENTS

Addison Wesley · Benjamin Cummings · Longman · Prentice Hall · Pearson Custom Publishing

Using Research Navigator
› Students
› Professors

Home | Research Process | Finding Sources | Using Your Library

You Are Logged In
Welcome, maria.
› Edit your profile
› Log Out

Additional Resources
› About
› Take a Tour
› Technical Support
› How to Adopt
› Visit our Publishers
› Feedback

Copyright
Pearson Education,
2002.
License Agreement
Privacy Policy

The New York Times
ON THE WEB

Search results for 'enron and (auditor or auditors)'

Match: [All ▼] Format: [Long ▼] Sort by: [Score ▼]
Redefine your search by adding terms:
[Enron,auditor] [Search] Search Tips

Documents 1 - 10 of 493 matches.

02/07/02
Thursday's Session of Hearing on Enron
Thefollowing is the full text of Thursday's session of a hearing of the oversight and investigations subcommittee of the House Energy and Commerce Committee on the findings of **Enron**'s special investigative committee as recorded by the Federal News Service. Witnesses: • Andrew Fastow, former chief financial ...

01/16/02
Investigators Question Fired Enron Auditor
WASHINGTON, Jan. 16 — Congressional investigators were interviewing a former partner of the accounting firm Arthur Andersen today about the destruction of paper and electronic documents related to the collapse of the **Enron** Corporation (news/quote). David B. Duncan, who had been the partner in charge ...

01/17/02
Auditor Received Warning on Enron Five Months Ago
WASHINGTON, Jan. 16 — **Enron** (news/quote)'s **auditors** knew in mid-August of a senior **Enron** employee's concerns about improprieties in the energy company's accounting practices, Congressional investigators studying **Enron**'s collapse said today. Officials of the auditing company, Arthur Andersen, sought ...

01/31/02
As Enron Searches for Auditor, Some Big Names Don't Apply
Firing its old **auditor** was easy. Now, with Arthur Andersen out of the way, the **Enron** Corporation (news/quote) faces a much more difficult task: finding another accounting firm willing to take its place. Two of the other four large accounting firms said they did not intend to compete for the account ...

Research Navigator

Back · Forward · Stop · Refresh · Home · AutoFill · Print · Mail

Address: http://www.researchnavigator.com/index.html · go

Products for Mac · Microsoft Internet Explorer · http://intranet.pearsoned.com/index.htm · Microsoft Outlook Express · Microsoft Office · Microsoft · Apple

Research Navigator.c⊛m
RESOURCES FOR COLLEGE RESEARCH ASSIGNMENTS

Addison Wesley · Benjamin Cummings · Longman · Prentice Hall · Pearson Custom Publishing

Using Research Navigator
› Students
› Professors

Home | Research Process | Finding Sources | Using Your Library

You Are Logged In
Welcome, maria.
› Edit your profile
› Log Out

Additional Resources
› About
› Take a Tour
› Technical Support
› How to Adopt
› Visit our Publishers
› Feedback

Copyright
Pearson Education,
2002.
License Agreement
Privacy Policy

The New York Times
ON THE WEB

Search results for 'enron or (auditor or auditors)'

Match: [Any ▼] Format: [Long ▼] Sort by: [Score ▼]
Redefine your search by adding terms:
[Enron,auditor] [Search] Search Tips

Documents 1 - 10 of 2798 matches.

02/07/02
Thursday's Session of Hearing on Enron
Thefollowing is the full text of Thursday's session of a hearing of the oversight and investigations subcommittee of the House Energy and Commerce Committee on the findings of **Enron**'s special investigative committee as recorded by the Federal News Service. Witnesses: • Andrew Fastow, former chief financial ...

01/16/02
Investigators Question Fired Enron Auditor
WASHINGTON, Jan. 16 — Congressional investigators were interviewing a former partner of the accounting firm Arthur Andersen today about the destruction of paper and electronic documents related to the collapse of the **Enron** Corporation (news/quote). David B. Duncan, who had been the partner in charge ...

01/17/02
Auditor Received Warning on Enron Five Months Ago
WASHINGTON, Jan. 16 — **Enron** (news/quote)'s **auditors** knew in mid-August of a senior **Enron** employee's concerns about improprieties in the energy company's accounting practices, Congressional investigators studying **Enron**'s collapse said today. Officials of the auditing company, Arthur Andersen, sought ...

01/31/02
As Enron Searches for Auditor, Some Big Names Don't Apply
Firing its old **auditor** was easy. Now, with Arthur Andersen out of the way, the **Enron** Corporation (news/quote) faces a much more difficult task: finding another accounting firm willing to take its place. Two of the other four large accounting firms said they did not intend to compete for the account ...

Chapter 6

Using Link Library

Link Library and the Web

Link Library is a collection of Web links, organized into 24 academic subjects, which are in turn divided into subcategories and lists of individual sites. The sites are editorially reviewed, which means that they have been selected because they offer credible and reliable information.

For example, if you were to select the "pollution" subcategory from the **Biology--Environmental Science** subject category, you would get a list of a dozen links. The site topics range from different types of pollution--air, noise, water--to the status of environmental legislation. How dependable are the sources? All are well-known and well-regarded government or educational institutions: the Environmental Protection Agency, NASA Ames Research Center, the University of California at Irvine. Some may quarrel with policies and enforcement efforts of government agencies, but the federal government has a long-established role in collecting data and disseminating information. The government websites listed here cover straightforward, non-controversial subjects: a definition of water pollution, how stratospheric ozone is being depleted, the latest city-by-city air pollution data, etc.

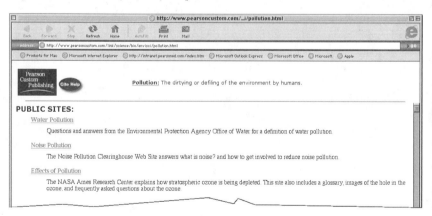

Suppose you look for the same information from websites listed by Yahoo! It turns out that many sites listed under "pollution" are from government and educational agencies. But you will also come across sites like one in which the author describes herself as "devoted to addressing the aspects of the environmental crisis left unacknowledged or inadequately addressed by the vast majority of existing environmental groups." The site is attractive, it doesn't solicit contributions, and it collects articles from generally well-regarded secondary sources, like the Associated Press. But its focus is on opinion, and lists topic headings such as "prophecy" and "prayer." It contains little of scholarly interest and no discernible research evidence. The site's author, while enthusiastic and well-intentioned, is not well-known or well-regarded.

In addition, the Web links in Research Navigator's Link Library are monitored and updated each week to reduce the chance of encountering "dead" links.

What's in Link Library?

Link Library echoes the variety of the World Wide Web. It offers images, text, government and academic documents and research, databases, and search engines. As with any subject directory, you need to narrow your search to the most useful category. You can find links to websites about AIDS, for example, in a half-dozen subject categories: biology, criminal justice, U.S. and world history, philosophy-ethics, and sociology. When you have selected a subject area and found the topic you are seeking, you will find a list of sites. The character of the site you choose to consult will often depend on your topic. The sites in Link Library can be:

- **Scholarly.** If you are researching photosynthesis and you go to the **Biology** subject area, you will find such sites as "What Is Photosynthesis?" and "Photosynthesis Research," maintained by Arizona State University. "Virtual Chloroplast," by the University of Illinois at Urbana-Champaign, contains an image of a chloroplast that lets you click on certain regions for more information.

- **Straightforward.** What if you want information on the 2000 presidential election but don't want to be flooded with opinion pieces about the disputed Florida results? Go to **Political Science – American Government > Presidential Elections**. It has sites such as "Atlas of U.S. Presidential Elections," with voting results for elections dating back to 1860; "U.S. Electoral College," the homepage for the National Archives and Records Administration Guide to the Electoral College; and "Elections," which provides graphs on electoral and popular votes for all U.S. presidential elections to date.

- **Controversial.** You're researching a topic that has heated arguments on both--or many--sides, and you want to summarize the range of public opinion. Link Library subject directories on such topics will lead you to a balanced variety of voices. Under **Philosophy–Ethics**, for example, you will find a list of "partial-birth abortion" links that include a pro-choice site, the text of the *Roe vs. Wade* decision, the National Right to Life Committee homepage, a site that attempts to provide all views of the issue, and a Planned Parenthood site that describes medical procedures performed at various stages of pregnancy.

- **Practical.** Want some help in finding sources on the Web? Go to the **Information Technology** subject directory. The "search engine" heading offers tips for effective Internet searching, common questions about how search engines work, and a chart to help you choose the best search engine for a task.

Finding Information with Link Library

To use this database, you choose a subject from the drop-down list, and, using the alphabetical directory, find the key term for the topic you are searching. Click on the key term and see a list of editorially reviewed websites.

Some topics with wide-ranging aspects appear under more than one subject heading. For example, a list of websites about alcoholism and alcohol abuse can be found under Criminal Justice, U.S. History, General Psychology, and Sociology.

Chapter 7

Using ContentSelect

About ContentSelect

EBSCO's ContentSelect Academic Journal Database is an archive of scholarly peer-reviewed journals and general interest periodicals. Thousands of articles and citations from general interest publications and prestigious academic journals can be instantly accessed in several ways using ContentSelect's search engine. Titles are chosen to reflect multiple perspectives in a range of topics, under 22 broad subject headings in the sciences, humanities, and social sciences.

Of course, ContentSelect is not a substitute for evaluation. Careful research studies sometimes contradict one another, and even authorities disagree. However, while many sources on the Internet may present questionable data or rely on dubious authorities to draw conclusions, ContentSelect provides a wealth of professionally-reviewed information that you can search and evaluate with confidence.

What's in ContentSelect?

ContentSelect offers searchable databases of academic journals and general interest publications. Academic journals are peer-reviewed; general interest publications are not.

Academic Journals

Rather than having a staff of writers who write something on assignment, journals accept submissions from academic researchers all over the country and the world. The journal editor then relies on "peer reviewers," or experts in the author's field, to evaluate the papers submitted to help determine if they should be published. The result is that the content of journal articles meets a higher standard than that of popular magazines, newspaper articles or Web pages. Journals provide specialized knowledge and information about a research topic and adhere to strict professional guidelines for methodology and theoretical grounding.

Scholarly journals are published several times per year. All the issues published in one calendar year constitute a volume. For example, the *American Sociological Review*, the journal of the American Sociological Association, published Volume 65 in the year 2000. That year's volume was made up of six individual issues, numbered Vol. 65 No. 1 and so on.

Additionally, journal issues may contain letters to the editor, book reviews, and comments from authors.

General Interest Publications

In addition to scholarly journals, subject databases--particularly the General Interest database--in ContentSelect include periodicals that are not peer reviewed. Some examples are *Commentary*, *Washington Monthly*, *Newsweek*, *USA Today Magazine*, and the *Christian Science Monitor*. These publications are included because they have articles that are generally credible and reliable. If your topic is timely or controversial, general interest publications may offer more appropriate coverage than academic journals.

Sometimes it's not easy to know at first glance which category a publication fits. For example, you find an article in *Science News*. Is that an academic journal, as the journal *Science* is? When you go to your subject database, click on the "publications" tab. You can scroll down to *Science News* or use the "browse" button to find it. When you click on *Science News*, you'll get an information box that describes the subjects it covers plus a characterization of its content: "presents articles of interest to scientists and others ..." The "and others" is a clue; then, when you check the "peer reviewed" section, it has an "N" for "no." So *Science News* is a general interest publication, not an academic journal. Still, any article in *Science News* is probably reliable, subject to the evaluation you conduct for all sources (see Chapter 2).

Searching ContentSelect

Select a Database

ContentSelect's homepage features a list of databases. To search within a single database, click the name of the database. To search in more than one database, hold down the alt or command key while clicking on the name of the database.

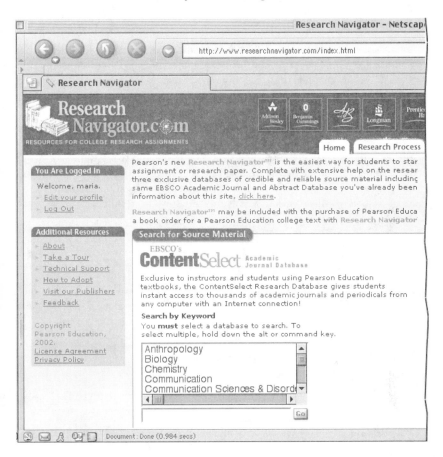

Basic Search

After selecting one or more databases, you must enter a keyword or keywords, then click on "go." This will take you to the basic search window. If you've selected a precise and distinctive keyword, your search may be done. But if you have too many results--which is often the case--you need to narrow your search.

The basic search window lets you create a search using a variety of search methods. Enter your search terms in the **Find** field and select from the available search modes: **standard, all words, any words,** or **exact phrase.**

Standard Search (Boolean)

- **And** combines search terms so that each result contains all of the terms. For example, search **SUV and conservation** to find only articles that contain both terms.

- **Or** combines search terms so that each result contains at least one of the terms. For example, search **SUV or conservation** to find results that contain either term.

- **Not** excludes terms so that each result does not contain the term that follows the "not" operator. For example, search **SUV not conservation** to find results that contain the term **SUV** but not the term **conservation.**

Using the above examples, suppose you were writing a paper about sport utility vehicles and energy conservation, in light of growing criticism of their low gasoline mileage. If you selected the "General Interest" database from ContentSelect and used the Boolean "or," at the time this was written, you would get 800 results for **SUV or conservation**. If you used the Boolean "and" option, (**SUV and conservation**) you would get only two results:

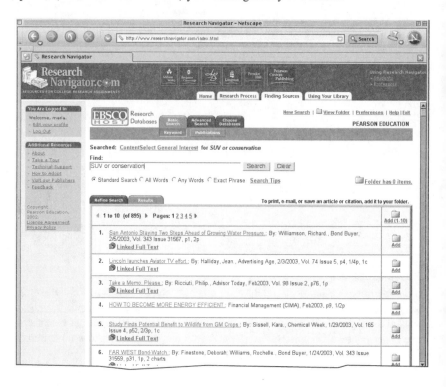

But suppose you decided to write about SUVs and didn't want articles that mentioned the energy conservation issue. If you searched for **SUV not conservation**, you would get 197 results:

Using "All Words"

In the "All Words" mode, ContentSelect conducts a Boolean search, assuming an AND between each word. The order of the search words entered does not matter. Any results that are displayed must include all words entered, regardless of how close they are to each other. Your search results are presented in order by date.

Using "Any Words"

"Any words" will return pages that include at least one of your terms-- equivalent to using the Boolean "or." For example, if you type in **SUV energy conservation**, you will get results that include one, two, or all three terms.

The more keywords that appear in an article, the more relevant the record is and the closer to the top of the results list it appears. What this means is that you can also enter a phrase or sentence that describes what you want to search for. Any results will appear in ranked order, with the most relevant article presented first.

For example, type **improving gas mileage for SUVs** to find articles that contain **improving, gas, mileage,** or **SUVs**. Prepositions such as **for** and articles such as **the** are excluded from the search. Results at the top of the list will have more (or all) of your keywords than results farther down the list.

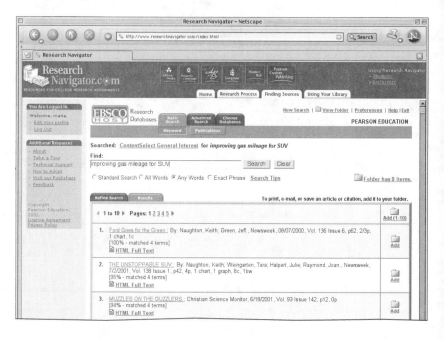

Using "Exact Phrase"

Enter the word or phrase that you want to find. Any results that are displayed will include all the words you entered, exactly as you entered them. (However, stop words--articles and prepositions--are still ignored.) Your search results are presented in order by date.

You can achieve the same results, clicking on any search method, by placing **quotation marks** around search terms. For example, type in **"gas mileage"** and click the "any words" option and you will get the same results you would by typing **gas mileage** and clicking the "exact phrase" option.

Advanced Search

On the tabbed tool bar, click **Advanced Search**. The advanced search window appears. Enter your search terms in the **Find** field. Your search terms can be keywords or selections from search history. Boolean operators (AND, OR, NOT) can also be included in your search.

You can also use **field codes** with your search terms. Fields refer to searchable aspects of an article or Web page; in the case of ContentSelect, they include author, title, subject, abstract, and journal name. Click **Field Codes** to display a list of field codes available with the databases you are using. Type the field code before your search terms to limit those words to the field you entered. For example, **AU Naughton** will find records that contain Naughton in the author field.

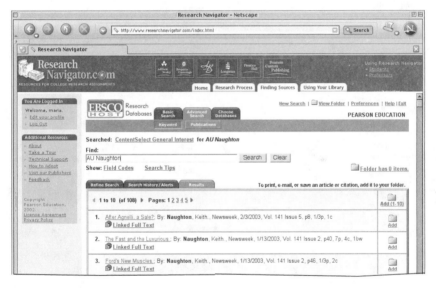

To **print, e-mail, or save** several search results, click on the folder next to the result; then print, e-mail, or save from the folder at the top of the results field. (You can still print, e-mail, or save individual results from the open article or citation.)

You can remove specific results, or clear the entire folder and collect new results, during your session. If you end your session, or it times out due to inactivity, the folder is automatically cleared.

Full Text Results

Some ContentSelect results will be available in full text--that is, if you click on the full text logo at the bottom of an entry, you will be able to call up the entire journal or magazine article. If you want to limit your search to results available in full text, click on the "search options" tab, and then on "full text." Then renew your search.

Abstract and Citation Results

Many ContentSelect results are in the form of citations containing abstracts. A **citation** is a bibliographic reference to an article or document, with basic information such as ISSN (International Standard Serial Number, the standard method for identifying publications) and publisher that will help you locate it. An **abstract** is a brief description of an article, usually written by the author. An abstract will help you decide whether you want to locate the work--either in an electronic database or a print version--through your college library.

A handy tip: once you have found an article that meets your research needs, you can search fields easily from the article citation to turn up similar articles. For example, suppose the *Christian Science Monitor* article "Gas-guzzling SUVs muster up a makeover" (Evarts, July 6, 2000) suits your paper perfectly. Go to the citation and click on the subject field to find similar articles. Or, if you want to see what else the author has written, click on the author field to produce a list of articles he has written.

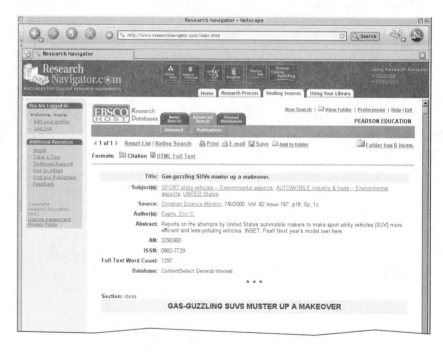

In many cases you can search the full text of articles using electronic databases and then read the entire article online. Typically, in order to use these databases you need to have a library card number or special password provided by the library. But sometimes when you use an electronic database you will find that the text of an article won't be accessible online, so you'll have to go to the library's shelves to find the magazine or newspaper in which the article originally appeared.

For more information, explore "Understanding the Research Process" and "Using Your Library" on the Research Navigator homepage.

Chapter 8

Using Research Navigator and the World Wide Web for Political Science Writing Assignments

Get used to it! Before your leave the ivy halls of academe and enter the "real world" of life, you will probably have to engage in a research writing assignment. Many students approach this academic requirement with a negative attitude. However, the job has to be done, just as a job will have to be done when you graduate from an institution of higher learning. In fact, one could say that your first research assignment could be an asset later on when you are required to submit formal reports and present information in a different professional setting.

However, you are indeed lucky! Unlike your parents of a generation ago, your job is a lot easier. If your parents wanted to secure various types of information for their term papers, they had to visit their college or university library, which might have been a traumatic experience for them--unless perhaps they were able to find a social advantage of doing so, such as a finding a date for the weekend. Of course, libraries are great for finding information relating to term papers (and for finding dates), but thanks to the computer era it is much easier and quicker to find valuable information for research assignments. This means that you can sit in your room and use the computer via Research Navigator and the World Wide Web. These "tools" will certainly provide you with an appropriate amount of information for your term paper.

Research Navigator is a fully online research service for academic needs. The site includes three databases for conducting research. The first is EBSCO's ContentSelect, which gives you immediate access to a multitude of academic journals and periodicals. The second is the *New York Times* digital archive. This searchable archive of *New York Times* articles and material can be browsed by keyword or subject matter and the articles found can be saved to the user's hard drive. The final service provided by Research Navigator is Link Library, a catalog of links to various websites that are organized by discipline and by key terms. The links provided here are constantly updated to ensure a low occurrence of dead links.

There are various ways to begin a research assignment. First, one should really consider choosing a topic that is of special interest. This means that you should enjoy finding information and reading about the subject matter. In addition, perhaps you may want to find a topic that relates to a future employment opportunity. For example, if you are planning on entering law school, you may want to research job opportunities for new lawyers. On the other hand, if there is a special area of interest relating to your political science class, such as "women in politics," you may want to write your paper about that.

After choosing a "special topic" it is a good idea to formulate an outline relating to it. This can be done by looking at the titles of a number of articles or books, and combining them into a coherent and logical summary of the topic. This would then result in a broad outline for your paper. However, leave a little room for possible changes in terms of additions or deletions to your paper because in your reading of appropriate sources perhaps new and additional interesting topics relating to your paper will come to your attention. Once you have your outline, which contains the main points of your paper, then take each main point and find several different commentaries about it from which you can secure information pertinent to the individual topic. Within a short period of time, you will find that you have enough information for all topics and your paper should have enough information in it.

In writing your paper, you will have to select a particular method or combination of methods to present the material. The methods vary and they can all be used. Select one that is most comfortable for you. A common approach of presenting the material is the historical approach. This means that you could start with the beginning of an event and then trace its evolution over time. Another popular event is that of the comparative approach. This means that you compare one event with another event looking for similarities and differences. Another approach is that of the behavior approach which uses statistical data to provide information. Of course, you could combine a number of approaches in your paper.

In writing your research paper, it is always a good idea to consult the syllabus for your course because an instructor often puts important information in it referring to a required term paper. This information could include the scope of topics, the length of the paper, and a particular style of referencing appropriate sources cited in the paper. If you do have a research assignment and your instructor does not have a written commentary regarding suggestions about it, it might be a good idea for you to discuss your approach in writing the paper with him or her. Not only will there be a chance that you might receive valuable hints about what the instructor believes to be important, but it might show your instructor that you are indeed interested in writing a worthwhile paper.

Of course, you will want to find out what style of writing is acceptable to your instructor. Many instructors suggest a popular work by Kate L. Turabian, *A Student's Guide to Writing College Papers*, published by the University of Chicago Press. This is what this author used during his graduate school days when he was writing political science papers. Another source could be *The*

Writer's Guide—Political Science by Arthur W. Biddle and Kenneth M. Holland with Toby Fulwiler, published by D. C. Heath and Company. In addition, you might want to consider *The Elements of Style* by William Strunk Jr. and E. B. White, and published by Macmillan. Indeed, do check with your instructor regarding an acceptable style of writing.

It might be a good idea for you to keep in mind that there are various degrees of sources in terms of appropriateness when writing papers. Specifically, there are primary or original sources of information, and then there are secondary sources of information. Primary sources of information are the best sources. They refer to the actual documents or statements relating to political events. For example, a copy of a federal law is much better than someone else's commentary about it. The copy of the federal law would be the primary source of information, whereas the commentary about it would be the secondary source. For example, if you read the Supreme Court's opinion about the very famous case of *Brown v. Board of Education* in its original form, this would be a primary source of information. If you read about the same case in your introductory political science course, and used that material to indicate what the Court did say, you would be using a secondary source. If you used an article from a newspaper, journal, or some book, it most likely will be a secondary source. Most of the time undergraduate students do not use primary sources and rely mostly of secondary sources. Yet, if you have a choice between a primary source and a secondary source, use the primary source because it will make your paper more professional.

In this chapter, we will be looking at four main areas relating to an introductory course in political science. One area is that of ideologies. Ideologies often motivate and explain the behavior governments. However, each government is usually divided into three main parts: the legislature, the judiciary, and the executive part. Thus, these parts are alluded to in this chapter.

Political Ideologies

Individuals within a society are often influenced by a particular ideology. Basically, an ideology is a system of beliefs often associated with the behavior of a government. Our society has experienced the effects of ideologies in several ways. For example, the advocacy of one type of ideology may result in government playing an active role in our society on a daily basis. However, another type of ideology or set of beliefs may encourage a more conservative reaction of government in its relation to citizens. In addition, some ideologies may have a positive connotation, while others may have a negative connotation. The purpose of this particular section is to identify for students a number of major ideologies that have impacted on our society, as well as to provide valuable websites which may be consulted to better understand their meaning and implications. It is important to note, however, that an ideology is subject to different interpretations. Not all individuals will define a particular ideology in the same way. There is certainly room for various views of an ideology.

Democracy

Democracy is perhaps one of the more popular types of ideologies. It has a very favorable connotation, and that may explain why it is so popular in many different countries. It is also one of the more difficult ideologies to define for writers. It is interesting to note that when many authors attempt to define it, they often quote someone else's definition. For example, one of the most often-quoted definitions is attributed to Abraham Lincoln, who is reported to have referred to it as government of the people, by the people, and for the people. Obviously, this is not the only definition, but it is one that is found in many works. However, the essence of democracy is an enhanced role of the citizens in the decision-making process of government. The term democracy is quite old and goes back to the ancient Greeks.

Many different countries like to refer to their system as a type of democracy. For example, the term "democracy" has often been cited by the Americans as a characteristic of the United States. In addition, the Russians have said the same thing in reference to their country when it was called the Soviet Union. Yet, when one examines how governments operated in both countries, there are obvious major differences. Consider just the example of free speech. In the United States, we have had a history of opportunity for our citizens to express themselves in many ways, including those that are unpopular. But in the former Soviet Union, citizens did not have as much opportunity to do so.

The following websites should be of value in attempting to obtain some basic understanding of democracy as an ideology.

> http://www.house.gov/donyoung/issues/US form of government 1999012 6.htm This source is a letter from a United States Congressman in 1999 giving an explanation of the meaning and implications of democracy as found in this country.

> http://ctl.idealog.info/democracy is the worst form of government.html This source starts out with an interesting quote from Winston Church which suggests that democracy is the worst form of government except for all those forms that have been tried. However, the author notes that despite its failings, democracy is the best form of government we can come up with when alluding to types of governments.

Liberalism as an Ideology

Liberalism as a form of ideology is another concept that has different meanings to individuals. Of course, it has been around for a long period of time. It suggests an active role by the government in terms of influencing citizens. In the twentieth century, Franklin Roosevelt exemplifies one who accepted this ideology. The numerous programs associated with his New Deal during the Great Depression are a strong indication of a liberal philosophy. Of course, not everyone will favor this particular ideology. For example, although a student may be in agreement with a liberal policy that brings about the opportunity to receive an educational loan, someone else whose taxes are raised to provide the loan may be opposed to this liberal policy of an active government influencing educational opportunities.

There are numerous websites that may be consulted to obtain more of an understanding of liberalism. Students may want to consider the following for additional information about this particular ideology:

http://fp.enter.net/~haney/liberalism.htm   This source indicates what liberals stand for. It also clarifies misconceptions about liberal intentions and outlines their values.

http://fp.enter.net/~haney/liberalism.htm This site notes that: *In a historical sense, liberalism can also be seen as the good and great of the only four truly high civilizations in world history: classic Greece, classic Rome, classic Europe, and classic America. All four of these confederations are long gone. This is so, even tho' the corpses and zombies of all four continue to exist, at least in some sense. But the ideas and spirit of these classic liberal societies live on.*

Liberalism can also be seen as the thought and spirit of the Age of Reason and the Enlightenment generally, particularly as manifested by Britain, France, and America around the cultural height of the planet: the late 1700s. Liberalism can be understood as the completely realized ideas, ideals, and culture of Burke and Smith, Voltaire and Diderot, Jefferson and Franklin. All of these individuals are the enlightened, uplifted product of an earlier radical English belief-system of nominalism, mechanicalism, materialism, empiricism, and reasonism. And these four noble intellectual institutions, in turn, were mostly created and elaborated by the Founding Fathers of the modern world: Francis Bacon, Thomas Hobbes, Isaac Newton, and John Locke. All were heroic Englishmen from the 1600s.

Finally, in contemporary terms, liberalism can be thought of as the correction, extension, and perfection of the two great proto-liberal movements of today: libertarianism and objectivism.

And if contemporary badly-compromised liberal democracy is truly the end of history governmentally -- as almost everyone says it is -- then pure cultural liberalism is the ultraend of history. Liberalism is the clear and definitive last word on, not merely politics, but philosophy, morality, esthetics, spirituality, and more.

Conservatism

Conservatism is another popular ideology. Like liberalism it has different meanings. However, in essence it suggests a restricted activity by the government in terms of making new policy. It is often cited as the opposite of liberalism. Perhaps one of the better known American political statesmen associated with it is that of the late Arizona Senator Barry Goldwater who authored *Conscience of a Conservative*. Conservatives are often more traditional in their view of society. They view the status quo as satisfying, and are less likely to see advantages in making major changes regarding public policy. In the United States, conservatives are often found in rural areas or the southern part of this country. Liberals, on the other hand, are often found in the northern part of the United States and especially in large northern cities where there is a great deal of diversity.

A number of sources are available which will provide you with additional information concerning conservatism:

> http://www.britannica.com/eb/article?eu=127641&tocid=0 will provide you with a commentary concerning conservative attitudes and varieties of conservatism. In addition, there is information about conservatism in the 20th century as found in various parts of the world such as Western Europe, Japan, and the United States.

> For an interesting commentary concerning conservatism and Associate Justice Clarence Thomas, who sits on the United States Supreme Court, see: http://college.holycross.edu/studentorgs/hcprelaw/clarence.html

> In addition, for a brief comparison of conservatism with other ideologies see the website: http://dspace.dial.pipex.com/town/street/pl38/sect2.htm

Totalitarianism

Totalitarianism as a concept could be considered the opposite of democracy. In the 20th century it is often analyzed in two different forms: fascism and communism. American democracy has experienced the challenges of both types. Totalitarianism has a number of obvious characteristics. For example, the role of the state is supreme to that of the individual. Second, there is a restriction in terms of freedom allowed for citizens who are subject to either type. Third, totalitarian systems often come into conflict with democratic systems of government. Sometimes these conflicts lead to war between or among various nation states, as was the situation during the 1940s.

Fascism

Early 20th century fascism is often associated with Benito Mussolini, the Italian political dictator. Of course, it is also associated with Adolph Hitler, the leader of Nazi Germany. A number of characteristics are often associated with fascism. For example, in fascist societies we find a strong sense of nationalism, a glorification of the state, and a willingness to use military force to obtain political objectives. In the case of Nazi Germany we also find a belief in the superiority of one race over other races. The United States has encountered both types and responded in a number of ways, including the use of its military. This was evident during World War II when this country fought the Italians while Mussolini was the leader of Italy, and when Hitler was the leader of Germany. A number of sources will provide you with additional information concerning fascism:

http://www.fordham.edu/halsall/mod/mussolini-fascism.html will give you Mussolini's definition of fascism, which he wrote for the Italian *Encyclopedia*. The article notes that "Mussolini came to power after the "March on Rome" in 1922, and was appointed Prime Minister by King Victor Emmanuel." Although we often think of Mussolini when studying fascism, the ideology was found in a number of other countries besides Italy. One source notes that "several countries embraced fascism between World War I and World War II. Some, such as Norway, Denmark, Great Britain, Belgium, and France, had large fascist movements. Others, such as Spain, Austria, Hungary, Rumania, Poland, and Finland, gained substantially fascist governments." See: http://www.kings.edu/history/20c/fascism.html

National Socialism (Nazism)

Another popular form of fascism is that of National Socialism or what is often referred to as Nazism. This particular ideology is associated with Adolph Hitler, the leader of Germany. It is similar to Italian fascism in some ways, but also differs. For examples, both types of fascism are associated with a dictator, and both emphasize the role of the state or nation over the individual. However, in Nazism we see a pronounced view of ethnic superiority with an emphasis on the Nordic race. In addition, Nazism is associated with a relentless pursuit of Jews and an attempt to bring about their liquidation from society, something not associated with Italian fascism.   A classic work relating to Nazism is that of *Mein Kampf* (My Struggle), written by Adolph Hitler while he served time in prison. It outlines his philosophy and views on various domestic and international matters.

For an interesting website which provides valuable information concerning German fascism, see: http://gi.grolier.com/wwii/wwii_hitler.html This website reviews the life of Adolph Hitler through various stages of his career. It details his early life, military service, political career, and rise to power.

For information about *Mein Kampf*, outlining Hitler's philosophy, students might want to view this site: http://www.stormfront.org/books/mein_kampf/index.html

Communism

Another popular form of totalitarianism is that of communism. However, this particular ideology does differ from fascism. For example, absent is the calculated persecution of Jews associated with German fascism. In addition, the belief in the superiority of a race is not associated with communism. In fact, communism advocates a classless society. Although fascism recognizes the value of capitalism in terms of allowing private ownership of the "means of production," this is a characteristic not associated with communism, which suggests that the nation-state should own those entities which produce the vital goods of a society. Communism is often associated with the former Soviet

Union and a number of other countries today such as China, Cuba, and North Korea.

Historically, a number of individuals have played a vital part in the advocacy of Communism. Foremost of the many are, of course, Karl Marx and Vladimir Lenin. Yet they did differ between themselves in a number of ways. For example, Marx believed that communism would naturally come about in a society. Lenin, however, did not accept this view as readily. He believed that to bring communism about, it had to be helped by a small group of dedicated individuals who would instigate a revolution in those countries where communism was not present. Hence, he felt there was a need for "professional revolutionaries." The difference between Marx and Lenin should not be surprising because most ideologies will change over time as a result of new conditions coming about. Of course, today communism is not as popular as it once was in Russia. The poor economic conditions which came about in the former Soviet Union as a result of the presence of communism helped lessen its significance and role. Yet, it still exists in a number of countries in various forms.

For additional information about communism as a form of ideology and other characteristics of it, students may consult a number of valuable resources such as:

http://encarta.msn.com/encnet/refpages/refarticle.aspx?refid=76157224
This site will provide information about various forms of communism, its leaders, philosophy, and activities in a number of countries.

http://www.marxists.org/archive/lenin/works/1914/jul/granat/ This site contains important information about Karl Max and his doctrines.

In addition, a valuable site concerning Vladimir Lenin is http://www.ex.ac.uk/Projects/meia/lenin/

Obviously, the ideologies of democracy, liberalism, conservatism, fascism, and communism are not the only ideologies which have impacted on the United States over the years. However, they are some of the major ideologies that students should have some knowledge about if they are to obtain an understanding of today's current national and international situations.

The Legislature as a Political Institution

A legislature is a body of individuals that performs many important functions. This particular body also is referred to as a parliament or a national assembly. Examples of legislatures would be the German Bundestag, the British House of Commons, the United States Congress, the Japanese Diet, the Mexican National Congress, and the French National Assembly. Although it is obvious that there are differences among various legislatures, certainly the United States Congress and the British Parliament are important examples because they serve as models for analysis and commentary and have been replicated to a large extent by a number of other countries.

For a valuable list of national legislatures and their names see: http://www.polisci.com/web/legis.htm This site will also help you find detailed information about each legislature listed on the site.

Perhaps the most widely recognized function of a legislature is that of making laws, which is not really an easy task, considering the fact that most bills do not become laws. A bill is a proposed type of legislation, whereas a law is a rule affecting society and its members in some way. However, the making of laws is certainly not the only function performed by a legislature. Just think of how President Bill Clinton felt when he was being investigated by Congress and threatened with impeachment. For information concerning President Bill Clinton and impeachment see: http://www.courttv.com/casefiles/clintoncrisis/guide.html

In addition, legislatures usually represent groups within a society. For example, elderly Americans are now putting pressure on Congress to enact new health care legislation. See the following websites for information about the role of pressure groups and congress regarding health care:

http://www.calnurse.org/cna/new1/wpost070599.html
http://www.awb.org/news/newsletter/0501/p11healthcare0501.htm

Legislatures also perform an oversight function by monitoring the operations of government agencies or government officials. Of course, you yourself can use the legislature by requesting that your particular legislator provide you with certain information that may be of value to you. Of considerable importance to many people is another function of a legislature, and that is the appropriation of money for various projects.

For information concerning functions of legislatures, see:

http://magnet.undp.org/Docs/parliaments/Concept%20Paper%20Revised%20MAGNET.htm#BASIC

Types of Legislatures

The United States government is characterized by having what is called a bicameral legislature, resulting from the famous Connecticut Compromise associated with the American Constitution. A bicameral legislature is one in which the legislature is divided into two separate bodies. In the United States this is called the Senate and the House of Representatives.

The length of time that one serves in a legislature varies among countries. There is also some difference of opinion as to how long a person should serve in the legislature. For example, some might argue that having limited terms would result in new individuals bringing different ideas to the legislature for consideration. However, others could point out that experience in a legislature is needed by members to adequately respond to pertinent concerns. In the United States members of the Senate are elected for six years on a statewide basis, but members of the House of Representatives are elected for two years from congressional districts.

Each state has two United States senators, but some states have more members in the House of Representatives than other states. In parliamentary systems there is no definite date for the popular election of members. In the United States, incumbency is quite an advantage and it is not unusual for an American legislator to retain a seat in the legislature. The concept of a bicameral legislature is also associated with forty-nine state governments in this country. Nebraska is the only state that differs, in that it has a unicameral or one-house legislature. Great Britain and most other countries also have a bicameral legislature. The English Parliament is composed of two parts: the House of Commons and the House of Lords. However, some countries do have a unicameral legislature. Examples of such countries are China and New Zealand.

See the following websites for information about bicameral legislatures:

http://www.wwnorton.com/wtp3e/ch13_comp_pers.htm

http://mirror.undp.org/magnet/Docs/parliaments/Legislative%20Chambers.htm

See the following website for comments concerning incumbency in national legislatures:

http://www.uwec.edu/petersgd/research/apsa98.pdf

Types of Legislative-Executive Relationships

There are two basic types of legislative-executive relationships. For example, the United States is characterized by having a presidential type of government. However, Great Britain and other countries have a parliamentary form of government. The existence of a presidential type of government like we have in the United States implies that the power to govern is divided among the three branches of government—the legislature, the judiciary, and the executive. This separation of powers characteristic is often associated with the political theorist Baron Montesquie, who wrote the classic work *The Spirit of the Laws*.

The concept of a government divided into three parts has the advantage in that no one part is going to completely dominate or influence the other two parts. However, an obvious disadvantage is what is often referred to as "gridlock." A good example of this occurring is when there is a disagreement between the legislature, which is controlled by one party, and the president, who is of another party.

Another type of legislative-executive relationship is that of a parliamentary government. A parliamentary system of government results in governmental authority being found in the legislature (a parliament) and in a cabinet headed by a prime minister. The cabinet directs the administration of a government and has responsibility for key decisions. Cabinet members obtain their positions by being selected from the majority party in the legislature (the House of Commons in England) after being recommended by the Prime Minister. An advantage of the parliamentary system is that it avoids the gridlock between the legislative and executive parts of the government. It also makes it quite clear as to who is responsible for a particular type of governmental policy or action.

For a commentary concerning Montesquie's *The Spirit of the Laws* see:

http://comp.uark.edu/~secarte/spiritoflaws.html

For a commentary concerning the advantages of a presidential form of government in contrast to a parliamentary form of government, see:

http://www.dartmouth.edu/~ppq/x98/x98point.html
http://www.libertas2000.net:81/gallery/insgineer/ideaPre.htm

Leaders in Legislatures

All legislatures have leaders. Some of the more common ones are the Speaker, the majority leader, the minority leader, and whips. The Speaker presides over a chamber or branch of the legislature and manages the session held by the entity. This is what occurs in the United States House of Representatives. The individual who holds that position is elected to it by the majority party and is often considered the most important or influential person in it. However, the Speaker of the British House of Commons is a non-partisan officer elected by the members.

Yet it is the individual who manages the regular business of the legislature who seems to receive the most publicity. This person is sometimes called a floor leader. In the United States this is the leader of the majority party in each branch, and this explains why the person is called the majority leader. Of course, there is also a minority party leader in each branch of Congress.

Another valuable individual who exercises a type of leadership activity is the "whip," a person in each branch who has responsibility for advising other members of pending legislation and who takes the initiative in gathering the members together to vote on a particular issue.

It is also interesting to note that a Prime Minister has a great deal of power in a parliament and can in effect cause the majority to vote for or against a particular issue. However, in the United States, the president does not have this power even if he is a member of the majority party in the legislature.

For an interesting source of information about how the President Putin is relating to legislatures see:

http://www.nixoncenter.org/publications/articles/5_26_00PutinRegions.htm

Committees and Legislatures

Legislatures generally rely on committees to do much of their work.   This is also important to note because it is in committees where most of the important decisions regarding legislation are made.   President Woodrow Wilson is reported to have said: "Congress in session is Congress on public exhibition whilst Congress in its committee rooms is Congress at work."   Both the United States Senate and House of Representatives have a number of permanent committees that have responsibility for considering a specific type of bill.   Other countries such as Germany and Italy have a fairly large number of committees associated with their legislature.   However, Britain and France have far fewer committees associated with their legislatures.

There are advantages and disadvantages of committee responsibility in legislatures.   Obviously, they result in specialization and division of work. Their presence also makes it possible for special-interest groups to often have considerable influence in the legislative process.   Yet, committees could impede the implementation of necessary laws needed for a country.   For example, one of the reasons why necessary and important civil rights legislation was so slow in coming about in the United States was the reluctance of committees to allow civil rights bills to become enacted into law.

For an interesting commentary about President Woodrow Wilson and his book, *Congressional Government*, see:

http://www.nixoncenter.org/publications/articles/5_26_00PutinRegions.htm

Characteristics of Legislators

Legislators are not typical of the citizens who make up their constituency in several ways.   In terms of education, they are usually college-educated and are likely to have graduated from the better schools.   In terms of financial characteristics, they are the wealthier individuals in society.   For example, the United States Senate has often been referred to as the "millionaire's club." This is understandable because the expense of running for election to the United States Senate is quite high, and it is not inexpensive to run for the United States House of Representatives.   In terms of race, the members usually represent the majority race in their country.   In terms of gender, it is obvious that legislators are generally male.   Of course, there are always some exceptions to these general characteristics, but they are indeed notable exceptions.

Limitations on Legislatures

Legislatures are not unrestricted in their activities.   Obviously, they can be influenced in several ways.   Public opinion is an important limitation.   A legislature must constantly be concerned about how its actions may be perceived by the public, especially when the citizens have the opportunity to express their views via the electoral process.   Of course, in some countries the judicial branch constitutes a limitation, as is the case in the United States.   For example, during the New Deal of the Franklin Roosevelt administration a number of laws passed by the legislature were declared unconstitutional by the United States Supreme

61

Court. The chief executive of a country may also limit the legislature. This is obvious with the threat of a presidential veto of legislation.

For a commentary concerning congress and state legislatures, see:

http://www.uwec.edu/petersgd/research/apsa98.pdf

The Future of Legislatures

Legislatures, like other important institutions, will change over time. This is due to a number of obvious reasons. For example, the needs of each country are always changing and legislatures have to recognize the importance of these changes. In addition, the needs of citizens as well as the expectations of citizens regarding government services are increasing. Thus, legislatures will be subject to more pressure to respond to these needs.

The Judiciary

Every major political institution has its unique functions and characteristics. This is especially evident with the judiciary, because what it does is to interpret the rules that affect not only government but its citizens as well. The judiciary performs several other important functions, but it is fair to say that it exists to render justice and serve as a moderator for disputes, which is sometimes called engaging in conflict resolution. The decisions of the judiciary are not always popular because in most disputes someone wins and someone loses. In addition, decisions often have wide consequences affecting millions of individuals for a long period of time. Although the judiciary is not completely independent, it is isolated from political pressures to some extent. This is more likely to occur when judges have tenure for life and cannot be voted out of office like a president or a member of a legislative body. On the federal or national level, judges are appointed for life. On the state level in the United States, judges receive their positions in a number of different ways, including that of being elected to office.

For an interesting commentary concerning rules and guidelines for judges, see:

http://www.newshare.com/west/guidelines.html

For information of a historical nature concerning the American judiciary, see:

http://www.uscourts.gov/about.html

The Power and Influence of the Judiciary

Alexander Hamilton noted that the judiciary has "neither force nor will, but merely judgment." To some this may suggest that it is a weak part of government. It is indeed true that the judiciary has had to depend upon others in some cases to enforce its decisions. A good example this occurred in 1957 when President Eisenhower had to enforce a federal judicial decision by the use of military force. It is also true that in some cases court decisions are ineffective because a number of individuals have chosen to ignore them. Yet, when one looks at the totality of court decisions, there is generally compliance even if such compliance at times is slow and sometimes incomplete.

For an interesting commentary concerning Alexander Hamilton and the judiciary, see:

http://www-unix.oit.umass.edu/~jbrigham/Fed78.htm

Interest in the Judiciary

Interest in the judiciary varies with the times. Interest is usually heightened when the judiciary is involved in making a decision which will have personal effects on individuals. Interest is also increased when the judiciary is involved with a particular case that receives a great deal of public attention such as the O. J. Simpson case. Millions of individuals throughout the world demonstrated an intense interest in the case, and it is still a topic of reference in current discussions and often cited in various books and articles concerning the judicial system.

Another time when there was increased public interest in the judiciary occurred in 1937 when President Roosevelt attempted to "pack the court," or increase its membership, because he disagreed with some of its decisions.

For matters of interest relating to the O. J. Simpson case, see:

http://www.wagnerandson.com/oj/OJ.htm

For an interesting commentary concerning President Roosevelt's attempt to increase membership on the Supreme Court in 1937, see:

http://www.gre.ac.uk/~wp05/courses/usa/articles/fdrsplan.pdf

Background of Judicial Employees

Obvious judicial employees are lawyers, prosecutors, and judges. These individuals are not typical of the average citizen. For example, they usually come from an affluent background. This is often necessary because the cost of meeting the educational qualifications needed to participate as an activist with the judiciary are high in terms of money and length of time needed to obtain the professional competence necessary to make a contribution. Of course, these judicial employees have devoted several years to professional development by attending institutions of higher education. In the United States, as well as in other countries, other characteristics of judicial employees are obvious. For example, they are more likely to be male, more affluent than the average citizen, and reflect the dominant racial ethnic group of their country. In addition, they are more likely to reflect conservative characteristics in terms of temperament and attitude.

Some people suggest that judges do not make law, but only interpret it. However, there is usually some discretion, especially in cases where the law is not clear, which permits a judge to make a decision that allows for a personal value system to have some effect in a case. Of course, a judge's action or inaction regarding a legal matter may affect compliance with a law. For example, if a judge renders a very light sentence in a criminal case, some citizens may not take the law very seriously. The laws that judges interpret emanate from a number of different sources. Some of the more obvious sources are constitutions, legislatures, administrative rulings, and executive orders. Of course, law also emanates from court decisions, as is quite evident in the United States when one considers the role of the Supreme Court in affecting activity and behavior in this country.

The law that is most likely to be known in this country is a result of England. It is sometimes referred to as Anglo-Saxon law. It emanated from England during the Middle Ages and was adopted by that country's colonies, which included the present United States. Of all countries, England has had the greatest impact on the judicial system of the United States. Some of its more obvious contributions are common law principles, the justice of the peace, the sheriff, and the constable. Some of these contributions are still visible today in a number of our states.

For information concerning the English judiciary, see:

http://www.eurolegal.org/ukengjud.htm

For information concerning the French judiciary, see:

http://www.eurolegal.org/ukengjud.htm

How Judicial Decisions Are Made

The procedure for making judicial decisions usually involves a number of steps. Knowledge of the facts involving an event is of paramount importance. This will help to decide if indeed a situation reaches the status of a "case." Should a case exist, it is necessary to know which law to apply to it. Then there should be a proper application of the law to the case.

One way of deciding a case is to use a method often used in the United States and in some other countries. It includes the reliance on precedent, or as it is often called, the rule of *stare decisis*. The essence of *stare decisis* is that a present case is decided on the basis of the most recent similar case. One of the advantages of deciding a case in this way is that it creates a certain amount of predictability for one involved in the legal process. On the other hand, *stare decisis* should not and has not always been followed by the courts. One reason for not adhering to it is that changes are often necessary. In addition, a prior decision may have had negative consequences for a society. For example in a landmark court case, *Plessy v. Ferguson* (1896), the United States Supreme Court legalized segregation, which lasted for a long time—until the case was unanimously reversed in *Brown v. Board of Education* (1954). The decision in the *Brown* case was influenced to a large extent by the use of sociological studies, which were of substantial value to one party in the case.

For landmark court cases and important legal concepts, see:

http://www.landmarkcases.org/

However, as valuable as the rule of precedent is, it is not used by all countries to the extent that it is used in the United States. For example, Germany and France use codes to help them decide cases more so than precedent. In these countries judges are expected to consult these codes, know them, and apply their regulations to court cases. In addition to these codes, additional rules have been formulated in these countries to help judges make the most professional decision in a court case.

Code law is often associated with Napoleon. He had a substantial impact on the judiciary by developing a code of law for France. His code was later imposed on those colonies that came under the domination of France. In the United States, the only state that has been noticeably impacted by Napoleon is Louisiana, reflecting its French cultural tradition. Under Napoleonic law there is less reliance on precedent, but more on statutes or codes in determining the outcome of a case.

For comments concerning the Napoleonic Code, see:

http://www.wikipedia.org/wiki/Napoleonic_Code

To determine how the Code Napoleon makes Louisiana law different, see:

http://www.louisiana-legal.com/history_louisiana_law.htm

Case Law Jurists versus Code Law Jurists

The most obvious of the judicial employees such as judges, prosecutors, and lawyers are trained in different ways. In the United States, lawyers graduate from a college or university and then go on to complete three years of demanding study in a law school, where they are instructed by law school professors. However, in countries that utilize code law, these types of individuals receive a more general type of education in a university. In addition, they are more likely to be generalists, as opposed to American judicial employees, who are more likely to be specialists.

For an excellent article about lawyers in different countries, see:

http://august1.com/pubs/articles/lawyers.htm

For a very informative article about preparing for a career in law in the 21st century, see:

http://www.law.ua.edu/bfair/prepare.html

The Structure of a Judicial System

A judicial system has various levels. The most obvious levels are courts of original jurisdiction and courts of appellate jurisdiction. Jurisdiction implies authority to hear a case. When a case is subject to original jurisdiction, this means that the case has not been heard or considered before in any type of lower court. In the United States, the court of original jurisdiction for important or serious cases involving federal law is that of the district court. A district court is often referred to as the trial court regarding a federal court case.

However, it is possible for a litigant to rise or appeal from the district court to a higher court—referred to as an appellate court. Assuming the case appears for consideration before an appellate court, that court is exercising what is called appellate jurisdiction. When a court is exercising appellate jurisdiction, this means that the case had been tried before in a lower court. It is not unusual for a country to have a number of appellate courts, and most countries allow at least one appeal, because it is always possible that a change in the decision made by a court of original jurisdiction should be changed. However, the court of last resort or the highest court is that of a Supreme Court. Understandably it is the most important court in the United States, because the effects of its decisions are significant.

Thus, looking at the United States court system we see three levels in its judicial system: First, we see the district court where a case starts out. It is the lowest of the three general federal types of courts. Every state has at least one federal district court, but some states have more, reflecting an increased workload. Above the district court is the U.S. Court of Appeals. There are three of them and their jurisdiction is larger than that of a district court—usually affecting a number of states. Above this level is the United States Supreme Court, the final arbiter of judicial controversies.

Other counties like Canada, the Philippines, and India also have a single supreme court. Still other countries will have a supreme court but it is referred to by a different name, such as Great Britain's Lords of Appeal in Ordinary. The decisions of a highest court are extremely important because their decisions affect the entire country and all of the citizens in it.

For important facts about the American judiciary formulated by the American Bar Association, see:

> http://www.abanet.org/media/factbooks/judifact.pdf

For information about court systems in various nations, see:

> http://www.ncsconline.org/D_KIS/info_court_web_sites.html#international

For information about the British legal system, see:

> http://august1.com/pubs/articles/lawyers.htm

Concerns of the Judiciary

When judges hold court they usually are interpreting two types of laws: criminal and civil. In society, it appears that most citizens are more interested in judicial matters involving criminal law, unless a case has a direct personal effect on them—especially if the case is going to affect them in some financial way such as lower taxes, lower drug prescription costs, or some other situation involving their own personal money. Perhaps this interest in criminal law and criminal cases explains why the media in many countries devotes so much of its news to comments about crime. Yet, criminal law concerns are less present in court than civil law concerns. The overwhelming majority of cases considered by the court are civil in nature. These cases deal with matters such as family situations (divorce, child support), contracts involving a business relationship of some type, torts (where someone is suing and asking for an award of some type), and property matters.

The Future of the Judiciary

The future of the judiciary will be, like most other political institutions, characterized by a number of changes. For example, new laws relating to activity that was not present a number of years ago have come about. A good example would be in relation to computer usage in various forms such as e-mail. New controversies will also be brought to the attention of the court for some type of decision. For example, cloning activity is already becoming a very controversial and novel issue. Of course, new technology in terms of communication, access to information, and analysis of evidence such as DNA types will continue to affect the role of the judiciary in our society. New types of individuals will also be more likely to be part of the judiciary. In particular, the number of women who actively participate in the judicial process as lawyers, judges, and prosecutors has already substantially increased in the last generation. All indications suggest that this trend will continue to grow in the near future. We are also more likely to see minorities in terms of race or ethnic background become associated with the judiciary in positions of prominence. Finally, let us not forget another matter that will be revisited by the judicial system: the rights and privacy of our citizens. These have been obviously impacted by the September 11th tragedy and will no doubt be a regular concern to the judicial branch because of contrary views regarding our government's new restrictions and increased activities to promote national security.

Two Types of National Leadership Forms

Parliamentary Leadership

Western democracies are characterized by having two types of national executive leadership. The oldest is that of the parliamentary type which originated in Great Britain. It was transferred to many of its colonies and has been replicated by various countries in Europe and other parts of the world. It obviously still remains a viable form of national political leadership.

The United Kingdom is the best example of parliamentarianism. Under the parliamentary system, executive power is shared among a political leader such as a prime minister, the cabinet, and a state leader such as a King or Queen, as is the case in Great Britain. The King or Queen usually has little actual political power other than perhaps performing ceremonial duties, but does appoint the major political executive—such as the prime minister, the chancellor, or a premier. However, the major political executive such as the prime minister really holds political power and receives that position because of support from the majority party in the parliament.

See this site for important links to government positions and offices in the United Kingdom:

http://www.psr.keele.ac.uk/area/uk.htm

For information concerning lessons of presidential leadership, see:

http://www.pfdf.org/leaderbooks/l2l/summer98/goodwin.html

For information about the current British Prime Minister, see the official website:

http://www.number-10.gov.uk/output/Page1.asp

Presidential Leadership

Presidential leadership is a newer type of an executive national political phenomenon. It originated at the American Constitutional Convention and evolved over time with many changes. This type of national executive leadership differs from that found in the parliamentary system where different individuals perform varying roles. Under the presidential type, the obvious important roles such as chief of state, chief of party, chief executive, and chief legislator, as well as a number of other important roles, are all performed by just one person--the President of the United States. The United States is the best-known example of presidential leadership. However, the form is practiced in a number of other countries such as the Philippines and Latin American countries. Although the presidential system has worked quite well in the United States, it cannot be said to have been that successful in some other places such as Latin America.

National political power is more dispersed in presidential type of leadership than it is in a parliamentary type. Basically, this implies that no one part of a government under a presidential form of leadership is able to completely dominate the policy-making process. This is because there are enough "checks and balances" built into the system to prevent this from taking place. For example, Congress can refuse to enact a president's bill into law, as we saw with President Clinton's attempt to bring about new health administration laws. Of course, the president can veto legislation passed by Congress, yet, this veto can be overridden by a two-thirds majority in each branch of Congress. Also, the Supreme Court can check the president as it did with Richard Nixon, or as it did with some of the major pieces of legislation passed by Congress but initiated by President Franklin Roosevelt during the New Deal of the 1930s. The concept

68

of checks and balances which is so evident in the United States, and which has been both praised and criticized, is not evident in the parliamentary system where there is a strong connection between the national executive leader such as the prime minister and the parliament which passes a law.

For information relating to Richard Nixon, see:

> http://gi.grolier.com/presidents/ea/bios/37pnixo.html

For information about Franklin Roosevelt's problems with the United States Supreme Court, see:

> http://www.spartacus.schoolnet.co.uk/USArooseveltF.htm

Similarities Between the Presidential and Parliamentary Types of Leaders

Both types of leaders have a number of common characteristics. For example, they must be cognizant of public opinion. Without the support of public opinion, their ability to bring about successful programs is limited to a large extent, and may lead to their downfall as a political leader. Both are also limited by the economic resources and economic conditions of their countries. In order to implement even popular programs, there must be an adequate source of income and a certain amount of expertise to bring about these programs. Both types of political leaders must also be cognizant of their country's military capabilities. For example, how many countries have the military capability to counter aggression by a major foreign country? Finally, both will be praised or criticized for the success or failure of their country's national policy, for they are viewed as responsible for implementing it as well as managing a huge bureaucracy.

When one examines national political executives, it is interesting that other similarities become evident. For example, although women in some cases—notably in England, India, and Israel, have occupied high positions of political power, the fact remains that national political leadership remains characterized by the male gender. The educational and social backgrounds of national political leaders are also similar. They tend to be well educated and come from the higher social classes of society as found in their country. They are often politically experienced in that they have served previously in some form of governmental position before rising to a top national leadership position. National political leaders also tend to be articulate and capable of expressing their views quite well in public. Finally, to attain their position of high national political leadership, they usually have to have majority support, either from the voters in their country or from their party in the parliament.

For an interesting commentary concerning women as political leaders, see:

> http://www.iadb.org/sds/doc/DominguezEnglish.pdf

Differences Between the Two Systems

There are a number of differences between the presidential system and the parliamentary system in terms of executive leadership. For example, in the United States, the president is personally elected by the voters of the nation. This is not true of the parliamentary system, where the prime minister is selected by the majority party found in the parliament. This would suggest that the president has a wider base of support and a different type of support than does the prime minister.

In addition, the cabinet in England, which is the source of much policy in the parliamentary system, is comprised of members who are elected from the majority party in the House of Commons. In fact, English cabinet members are typically members of the majority party in the parliament. In the United States, cabinet members are nominated or appointed by the president and confirmed by the Senate. In addition, they are not usually members of the legislature—the Congress.

It is also interesting to note that the United States' president can be voted out of office by the voters, such as occurred with Presidents Gerald Ford and Jimmy Carter. However, in a parliamentary system as found in England, the prime minister can be forced out of office as a result of losing support from the majority party in the parliament.

Of course, under a presidential system there is more of a chance of difficulties relating to policy formation than there is in a parliamentary system. This is due to the fact that in the presidential system, a system of checks and balances exist among the branches of government. Thus there is a chance for so-called "gridlock" to develop in a presidential system. This is especially evident when the president is of one party and the Congress is controlled by a different party. Gridlock is lessened considerably in the parliamentary system because of the connection between the executive authority (the prime minister and the cabinet) and the majority of those serving in the parliament.

In addition, it is often more difficult to place responsibility for policy failures in a presidential system because the President can blame Congress for the failure, and Congress can turn around and blame the President. However, this is less true in the parliamentary system because the parliament is more closely allied with the cabinet in terms of policy support.

For information concerning Governing Systems and Executive-Legislative Relations, see the excellent commentary at:

http://magnet.undp.org/docs/parliaments/governing%20system.htm

For information concerning gridlock between Congress and the President, see:

http://www.usatoday.com/news/washington/2002-09-26-budget-gridlock_x.htm

The Future of National Political Leaders

National political leaders will see a number of changes in the future because the world is constantly changing. In particular, the activity of terrorist groups will present new challenges. This means that more resources will need to be allocated to counter this problem. Also, as we see an increase in the division between the rich and poor in society, new demands will be placed leaders to attempt to bring about a more equitable distribution of the economic wealth in their countries. The globalization taking place in the world will also force leaders to become more cognizant of the interdependence among nations. Public attention will also be more focused on national leaders, not only because of an increasing importance of their role in society, but also because of new technological developments which bring attention to their reactions in responding to new national and international problems.

For information about presidential leadership and the global environment, see:

http://pro.harvard.edu/PRO/papers/047/047002SussmanGle.pdf

For an interesting commentary concerning political behavior in terms of leaders and followers, see:

http://www.grazian-archive.com/politics/PolBehavior/C_03.html

Appendix A

Documenting Your Electronic Sources

Copyright laws came into effect when people started realizing that income could be made by selling their words. In an era dubbed "The Age of Information," knowledge and words are taking on more significance than ever. Laws requiring writers to document or give credit to the sources of their information, while evolving, are still in effect.

Various organizations have developed style manuals detailing, among other style matters, how to document sources in their particular disciplines. For writing in English composition and literature, Modern Language Association (MLA) and American Psychological Association (APA) guidelines are the most commonly used, but others, such as those in *The Chicago Manual of Style* (CMS), are available. Always find out from your instructor what style to use in a specific assignment so that you can follow the appropriate guidelines.

For general information on MLA and APA citations, the best print sources are:

> Gibaldi, Joseph. MLA Handbook for Writers of Research Papers. 5th ed. NY: MLA, 1999.

> American Psychological Association. (2001). *Publication Manual of the American Psychological Association* (5th ed.). Washington: APA.

Because the methods of obtaining electronic information are developing so rapidly, printed style manuals have had difficulty in keeping up with the changes and in developing documentation styles for electronic sources. As a result, the most up-to-date information from the MLA and the APA about documenting online sources with URLs can be found on these organizations' websites. This Appendix shows you how to credit your electronic sources based on the information there.

When you cite electronic sources, it is vital to type every letter, number, symbol, and space accurately. Any error makes it impossible to retrieve your source. Since electronic sources tend to be transitory, printing a hard copy of your sources will make it easier for you to cite accurately and provide evidence for your documentation. MLA style encloses Internet addresses and URLs (Uniform Resource Locators) in angle brackets < >. If you see them around an address, do not use them as part of the address when you attempt to retrieve the source. APA style does not enclose URLs.

Modern Language Association (MLA) Style Guidelines

These guidelines follow the documentation style authorized by the Modern Language Association for electronic sources. Web sources are documented in basically the same way as traditional sources. According to the MLA website, the following items should be included if they are available:

1. Name of the author, editor, compiler, or translator of the source (if available and relevant), reversed for alphabetizing and followed by an abbreviation, such as ed., if appropriate
2. Title of a poem, short story, article, or similar short work within a scholarly project, database, or periodical (in quotation marks); or title of a posting to a discussion list or forum (taken from the subject line and put in quotation marks), followed by the description Online posting
3. Title of a book (underlined)
4. Name of the editor, compiler, or translator of the text (if relevant and if not cited earlier), preceded by the appropriate abbreviation, such as ed.
5. Publication information for any print version of the source
6. Title of the scholarly project, database, periodical, or professional or personal site (underlined); or, for a professional or personal site with no title, a description such as Homepage
7. Name of the editor of the scholarly project or database (if available)
8. Version number of the source (if not part of the title) or, for a journal, the volume number, issue number, or other identifying number
9. Date of electronic publication, of the latest update, or of posting
10. For a posting to a discussion list or forum, the name of the list or forum
11. The number range or total number of pages, paragraphs, or other sections, if they are numbered
12. Name of any institution or organization sponsoring or associated with the website
13. Date when the researcher accessed the source
14. Electronic address, or URL, of the source (in angle brackets)

Examples:

Book
Shaw, Bernard. Pygmalion. 1912. Bartleby Archive. 6
    Mar. 1998 <http://www.columbia.edu/acis/
    bartleby/shaw/>.

Poem
Carroll, Lewis. "Jabberwocky." 1872. 6 Mar. 1998.
    <http://www.jabberwocky.com/carroll/jabber/
    jabberwocky.html>.

Article in a Journal
Rehberger, Dean. "The Censoring of Project #17:
    Hypertext Bodies and Censorship." Kairos 2.2
    (Fall 1997): 14 secs. 6 Mar. 1998 <http://
    english.ttu.edu/kairos/2.2/index_f.html>.

Article in a Magazine
Viagas, Robert, and David Lefkowitz. "Capeman Closing
    Mar. 28." Playbill 5 Mar. 1998. 6 Mar. 1998
    <http://www1.playbill.com/cgi-bin/plb/news?cmd
    =show&code=30763>.

Article in a Newspaper
Sandomir, Richard. "Yankees Talk Trades in Broadcast
    Booth." New York Times on the Web 4 Dec. 2001. 5
    Dec. 2001 <http://www.nytimes.com/pages/
    business/media/index.html>.

Article in a Reference Database
"Jupiter." Britannica Online. Vers. 97.1.1 Mar. 1997.
    Encyclopaedia Britannica. 29 Mar. 1998 <http://
    www.eb.com:180>.

Posting to a Discussion List
Grumman, Bob. "Shakespeare's Literacy." Online
    posting. 6 Mar. 1998. Deja News. <humanities.
    lit.author>.

Scholarly Project
Voice of the Shuttle: Web Page for Humanities
    Research. Ed. Alan Liu. Mar. 1998. U of
    California Santa Barbara. 8 Mar. 1998
    <http://humanitas.ucsb.edu/>.

Professional Site
The Nobel Foundation Official Website. The Nobel
    Foundation. 28 Feb. 1998 <http://www.nobel.se/>.

Personal Site
Thiroux, Emily. Home page. 7 Mar. 1998
    <http://academic.csubak.edu/home/acadpro/
    departments/english/engthrx.htmlx>.

Government or Institutional Site
Zebra Mussels in Vermont. Homepage. State of Vermont
   Agency of Natural Resources. 3 May 1998 <http://
   www.anr.state.vt.us/dec/waterq/smcap.htm>.

Synchronous Communications (such as MOOs, MUDs, and IRCs)
Ghostly Presence. Group Discussion. telnet 16 Mar.
   1997 <moo.du.org:8000/80anon/anonview/1
   4036#focus>.

Gopher Sites
Banks, Vickie, and Joe Byers. "EDTECH." 18 Mar. 1997
   <gopher://ericyr.syr.edu:70/00/Listservs/EDTECH/
   README>.

FTP (File Transfer Protocol) Sites
U.S. Supreme Court directory. 6 Mar. 1998
   <ftp://ftp.cwru.edu/U.S.Supreme.Court/>.

Online Work of Art
Van Gogh, Vincent. The Olive Trees. 1889. Museum of
   Modern Art, New York. 5 Dec. 2001 <http://
   www.moma.org/docs/collection/paintsculpt/
   recent/c463.htm>.

Online Interview
Plaxco, Jim. Interview. Planetary Studies Foundation.
   Oct. 1992. 5 Dec. 2001 <http://www.planets.org>.

Online Film or Film Clip
Columbus, Chris, dir. Harry Potter and the Sorcerer's
   Stone. Trailer. Warner Brothers, 2001. 5 Dec.
   2001 <http://hollywood.com>.

Electronic Television or Radio Program
Chayes, Sarah. "Concorde." All Things Considered.
   Natl. Public Radio. 26 July 2000. 7 Dec. 2001
   <http://www.npr.com/programs/atc/archives>.

Synchronous Communication
Author's last name, First name. Identifying label.
   "Title of work." xx Month 20xx. Name of forum.
   xx Month 20xx. <Telnet://lingua.networkname>.

Generally follow the guidelines for other online citations, modifying them
wherever necessary, but always provide as much information as possible. Some
cited material will require identifying labels (e.g., Interview or Online posting),
but such labels should be neither underlined nor set within quotation marks.
When documenting synchronous communications that are posted in MOO
(multiuser domain, object oriented) and MUD (multiuser domain) forums, name

the speaker or speakers; describe the event; provide the date of the event and the name of the forum (e.g., linguaMOO); and cite the date of access as well as the network name (including the prefix Telnet://).

Work from an Online Service

```
Author's last name, First name. Publication. 20xx.
     Internet Provider name. xx Month 20xx. Keyword:
     Name.
```
Or
```
Last name, First name. Publication. 20xx. Internet
     Provider name. xx Month 20xx. Path: Name; Name;
     Name.
```

```
Brash, Stephen B. "Bioprospecting the Public Domain."
     Cultural Anthropology 14.4 (1999): 535-56.
     ProQuest Direct. Teaneck Public Library,
     Teaneck, NJ. 7 Dec. 1999 <http://proquest.
     umi.com>.
```
Or
```
Dutton, Gail. "Greener Pigs." Popular Science 255.5
     (1999): 38-39. ProQuest Direct. Teaneck Public
     Library, Teaneck, NJ. 7 Dec. 1999 <http://
     proquest.umi.com>.
```

For works that have been accessed through an online service, either through a library service (e.g., ProQuest Direct or Lexis-Nexis) or through one of the large Internet providers (e.g., America Online), you may not know the URL of the source. In such cases, cite the keyword or path that led to the source, if applicable, and separate each individual item in the path with a semicolon; the keyword or path will be the last item in the citation. For sources accessed through library services, as above, cite the name of the service, the name of the library, the date you assessed the material, and the URL of the service's homepage. If you also know the name of the database used, include that information (underlined) before the name of the online service.

American Psychological Association (APA) Style Guidelines

The most recent (5th) edition of the *Publication Manual of the American Psychological Association* includes general guidelines for citing electronic sources, and the APA has published specific examples for documenting Web sources on its Web page. Go to:

http://www.apastyle.org/elecre.html

In general, document these sources as you do traditional sources, giving credit to the author and including the title and date of publication. Include as much information as possible to help your reader to be able to retrieve the information. Any sources that are not generally available to your readers should be documented within the body of your writing as a personal communication but not included in your reference list. Such sources include material from listservs, newsgroups, Internet relay chats (IRCs), MOOs, MUDs, and e-mail.

According to information at the website for the American Psychological Association entitled "How to Cite Information From the World Wide Web," all references begin with the same information that would be provided for a printed source (or as much of that information as possible). The Web information is then placed at the end of the reference. It is important to use the "Retrieved from" and the date because documents on the Web may change in content, move, or be removed from a site altogether. To cite a website in text (but not a specific document), it's sufficient to give the address (e.g., http://www.apa.org) there. No reference entry is needed.

Use the following guidelines to include a source in your reference list:

```
Name of author [if given]. (Publication date) [in
    parentheses]. Title of the article [following
    APA guidelines for capitalization]. Title of
    periodical or electronic text [italicized].
    Volume number and/or pages [if any]. Retrieved
    [include the date here] from the World Wide Web:
    [include the URL here, and do not end with a
    period]
```

Examples:

Journal Article
```
Fine, M. A. & Kurdek, L. A. (1993, November).
    Reflections on determining authorship credit and
    authorship order on faculty-student
    collaborations. American Psychologist, 48.11,
    1141-1147. Retrieved March 6, 1998 from the
    World Wide Web: http://www.apa.org/journals/
    amp/kurdek.html
```

Newspaper Article
```
Murray, B. (1998, February). Email bonding with your
    students. APA Monitor [Newspaper, selected
    stories online]. Retrieved March 6, 1998 from
    the World Wide Web: http://www.apa.org/monitor/
    bond.html
```

World Wide Web Site
Williams, Scott. (1996, June 14). Back to school with the quilt. *AIDS Memorial Quilt Website*. Retrieved June 14, 1996, from http://www.aidsquilt.org/newsletter/stoires/backto.html

File Transfer Protocol (FTP), Telnet, or Gopher Site
Altar, T.W. (1993). *Vitamin B12 and vegans*. Retrieved May 28, 1996, from ftp://ftp.cs.yle.edu

King, Jr., M.L. (1963, August 28). I have a dream [speech]. Retrieved January 2, 1996, from telnet://ukanaix.cc.ukans.edu

Synchronous Communications (MOO, MUD, IRC)
Harnack, A. (1996, April 4). Words [Group discussion]. Retrieved April 5, 1996, from telnet://moo.du.org/port=8888

Web Discussion Forum
Holden, J.B. (2001, January 2). The failure of higher education [Formal discussion initiation]. Message posted to http://ifets.mtu.edu/archives

Listserv (electronic mailing list)
Weston, Heather (2002, June 12). Re: Registration schedule now available. Message posted to the Chamberlain Kronsage dormitory electronic mailing list, archived at http://listserv.registrar.uwsp.edu/archives/62.html

Newsgroup
Hotgirl (2002, January 12). Dowsing effort fails. Message posted to news://alt.science.esp3/html

Appendix B

Glossary

Boolean Comes from the ideas of British mathematician George Boole (1815-1964). From his writings come the Boolean operators: AND, OR, and NOT, used to link words and phrases for more precise queries for search engines and directories.

Database A repository of information that is searchable.

Domain One of the different subsets of the Internet. The suffix found on the host name of an Internet server defines its domain. For example, the host name for Prentice Hall, the publisher of this book, is www.prenhall.com. The last part, .COM, indicates that Prentice Hall is a part of the commercial domain. Other domains include .MIL for military, .EDU for education, .ORG for non-profit organizations, .GOV for government organizations, and many more.

Download The process of transferring a file, document, or program from a remote computer to a local computer. (See Upload.)

E-mail The short name for electronic mail. E-mail is sent electronically from one person to another. Some companies have e-mail systems that are not part of the Internet. E-mail can be sent to one person or to many different people.

Homepage In its specific sense, this refers to a Web document that a browser loads as its central navigational point to browse the Internet. It may also be used to refer to as a Web page describing an individual. In the most general sense, it is used to refer to any Web document.

Host Another name for a server computer. (See Server.)

HTML This is an abbreviation for HyperText Markup Language, the common language used to write documents that appear on the World Wide Web.

HTTP An abbreviation for HyperText Transport Protocol, the common protocol used to communicate between World Wide Web servers.

79

Link A text element or graphic within a document that has an embedded connection to another item. Web pages use links to access documents, images, sounds, and video files from the Internet, other documents on the local Web server, or other content on the Web page. Hyperlink is another name for link.

Multimedia As a general definition, multimedia is the presentation of information by multiple media formats, such as words, images, and sound. Today, it is more commonly used to refer to presentations that use a lot of computer technology.

Nesting The use of parentheses to combine several search statements into one search statement.

Paraphrasing To restate in your own words a passage written or spoken by another person.

PDF This stands for Portable Document Format. It is a file format that allows authors to distribute formatted, high-resolution documents across the Internet. A free viewer, Adobe Acrobat Reader, is required to view PDF documents.

Plagiarism To present another person's words or ideas as if they were your own.

Primary Source Firsthand evidence, based on your own or someone else's original work or direct observation.

Search Engine An online service or utility that enables users to query and search the Internet for user-defined information. They are typically free services to the user.

Secondary Source To report describe, comment or analyze the experiences of work of others. A secondary source is at least once removed from the primary source.

Server A software program used to provide, or serve, information to remote computers. Servers function in a Client-Server information exchange model. This term may also be loosely applied to the computer that is used to serve the information.

Summarizing To condense the essentials of someone else's thoughts into a few statements. A summary is shorter than a paraphrase and provides only the main point from the original source.

Truncate To use a root of a word followed by an asterisk in order to retrieve variants of the word.

Upload The process of moving or transferring a document, file, or program from one computer to another computer.

URL An abbreviation for Universal Resource Locator. It is basic sense, it is an address used by people on the Internet to locate documents. URLs have a common format that describes the protocol for information transfer, the host computer address, the path to the desired file, and the name of the file requested.

Viewer A program used to view data files within or outside a browser.

Web (WWW) This stands for World Wide Web. When loosely applied, this term refers to the Internet and all of its associated incarnations, including Gopher, FTP, HTTP, and others. More specifically, this term refers to a subset of the servers on the Internet that use HTTP to transfer hyperlinked documents in a page-like format.

Web page A single file as viewed within a Web browser. Sever Web pages linked together represent a website.

References

Chapter 1

Barstow, D., & Bergman, L. (2003, January 9). A family's fortune, a legacy of blood and tears. *The New York Times*, p. A1.

Holland, E.I.M., Ph.D. (1997). *From the Mississippi Delta: A Memoir.* New York: Simon & Schuster.

Troyka, L.Q. (2002). *Simon & Schuster Handbook for Writers* (6th ed.). Upper Saddle River, NJ: Pearson Education.

Chapter 2

The Basics of Google Search. (2002). Retrieved February 27, 2003, from http://www.google.com/help/refinesearch.html

Finding Information on the Internet: A Tutorial. (2002). Retrieved January 14, 2003, from http://www.lib.berkeley.edu/TeachingLib/Guides/Internet/Strategies.html

Gallagher, D. F. (2002, December 9). In the 'Google' economy,' businesses thrive by appearing prominently on the search engine's free listings. *The New York Times*, p. E1.

Global Warming: Fact vs. Myth. (2001). Retrieved March 3, 2003, from http://www.environmentaldefense.org/documents/382_myths.htm

Internet Searching Tools. (2002). Retrieved February 27, 2003, from http://www.sou.edu/library/searchtools

Searching FAQs. (2003). Retrieved February 26, 2003, from http://www.cln.org/searching_faqs.html

Sullivan, D. (2001, October 26). Search engine math. *Search Engine Watch*. Retrieved January 13, 2003, from http://searchenginewatch.com/facts/math.html

Cohen, L. B. (2003). Internet tutorials. *University at Albany Libraries*. Retrieved January 11, 2003, from http://library.albany.edu/internet

Whalen, J. (2002, October 30). Explaining the recent Yahoo/Google changes. *Traffick.com*. Retrieved February 26, 2003, from http://www.traffick.com/article.asp?aID=120

Chapter 3

Chokshi, M., Carter, C., Gupta, D., Martin, T., & Allen, R. (1991). Computers and the apartheid regime in South Africa. *South Africa. Guide to Internet Resources. Stanford University*. Retrieved Dec. 12, 2002, from http://www-cs-students.stanford.edu/~cale/cs201

Goldstein, N. (Ed.). (1998) *The Associated Press Stylebook and Libel Manual*. Reading, MA: Addison-Wesley.

Halberstam, D. (2002, May 20). A Pulitzer Prize-winner speaks of terrorism, life after college and choosing wisely. *USC Chronicle, 21*(29), 10-11.

Sollee, D. (2001). *Smart Marriages. The Coalition for Marriage, Family and Couples Education*. Retrieved December 12, 2002, from http://www.smartmarriages.com/divorcepredictor.html

Troyka, L.Q. (2002). *Simon & Schuster Handbook for Writers* (6th ed.). Upper Saddle River, NJ: Pearson Education.

Chapter 5

New York Times Newspaper 2001 Fact Book. (2003). Retrieved February 16, 2003, from http://www.nytco.com/company-factbook.html

Chapter 7

Evarts, E. C. (2000, July 6). Gas-guzzling SUVs muster up a makeover. *Christian Science Monitor*.